GLASS
PAINTING
PROJECTS

GLASS
PAINTING
PROJECTS

DECORATIVE GLASS FOR
BEAUTIFUL INTERIORS

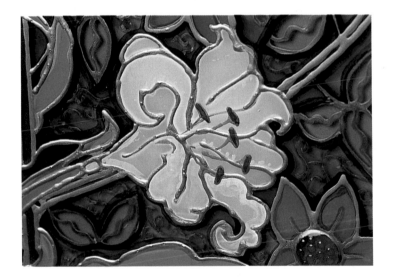

JANE & JOHN
DUNSTERVILLE

DAVID & CHARLES

DEDICATION

This book is for Dunstervilles and Munros all around the world,
especially our nephews and nieces, and Mollie Munro.

AUTHORS' ACKNOWLEDGEMENTS

Jane and John would like to thank all the following friends and associates for their enthusiasm and generous help
with the writing of this book:
Our son and daughter, Guy and Hannah Dunsterville, who both contributed to the concept, ideas, design
reference, expertise and practical skills in producing samples and finished drawings. Ted and Kate Barber, who
kept everything else going while we were all shut away in the Ivory Tower. Thameswey Homes for their very
considerable kindness in allowing us to photograph in their beautiful showhomes at Halsey Park, Hemel
Hempstead. Ken Lumsden of Designs in Wood, for the specialist blanks he cut in MDF, when he was already too
busy! All those customers, past and present, who were prepared to allow us to disrupt their lives with our
photography, especially the Longstaff family – Tony, Susan, Charlotte, Alexandra, Oliver and Henrietta – Claire
Rose, Patricia and Chris Rae, Brian and Judith Legg and Harry and Vicky Chadbone. All the craft show visitors
and mail order customers, whose questions formed the core of this book. We are especially indebted to Rodney
Burn and family for whom we developed the delightful and innovative idea of the chess table. And finally, Fiona
Eaton, for guiding the book through all the processes so smoothly.

Noah's Fludde on page 6 is from the authors' personal collection of glass painting work.

A DAVID & CHARLES BOOK

First published in the UK in 1998

Text and designs Copyright © Jane & John Dunsterville
Photography and layout Copyright © David & Charles

Jane & John Dunsterville have asserted their right to be identified as authors of this work in
accordance with the Copyright, Designs and Patents Act, 1988.

A catalogue record for this book is available from the British Library.

ISBN 0 7153 0833 5

Designer: Sue Michniewicz
Photographer: Karl Adamson
Stylists: Jo Harris, Maria Kelly

Printed in Italy by New Interlitho SpA
for David & Charles, Brunel House, Newton Abbot , Devon

CONTENTS

INTRODUCTION

Suddenly, coloured glass seems to be everywhere! A whole new generation of glass-painting materials has made the beauty of pure colour more accessible to the craftworker, creating demand for information, so it is no wonder that we are increasingly being asked how these materials can be used most effectively, how they should be applied and what aftercare they require.

This book is designed to answer as many of those questions as possible, and more. All the techniques required for successfully creating the many beautiful projects it contains are fully explained and illustrated, supported by practical advice and helpful tips. Once the basics, which are conveniently grouped in a comprehensive section at the beginning have been mastered, beginner and skilled practitioner alike will be able to complete any of the projects. These range from simple decorative features for any part of the home to more adventurous projects, including the creation of major focal features such as doors and windows. And there is nothing to stop the enthusiast from adapting projects, or even creating their own.

Modern glass paints are designed to overcome the obstacles presented by traditional methods, and much of their charm lies in the fact that they are readily accessible to the average household, as they are easily found in many good DIY stores and craft shops. Only the simplest of equipment is required for glass painting, and even a large project such as a glass panel for a front door will fit comfortably on a kitchen table and can be cleared away in minutes.

If you are ready to master the basics of glass painting and apply them to create beautiful and exciting projects this informative, practical sourcebook will assure success and lasting pleasure.

'copper-foiling' was also his invention, allowing curved and three-dimensional shapes to be created for his stunning range of lampshades in jewel colours.

MACKINTOSH

A lasting influence has been the stained glass work of the renowned Glasgow architect Charles Rennie Mackintosh, which owes much to the designs of his wife Margaret. Working together, they produced sinuous, flowing shapes derived from Japanese art forms, including their well-loved rose motif. Colours were more muted, and the lead line took on a greater significance in the design. The strong vertical emphasis and emerging geometric shapes foreshadow the early Art Deco style.

EDWARDIAN

Edwardian style was grand and imposing, befitting a time of great confidence and prosperity. Windows were generally larger, indicating a preference for light, airy interiors. Under the influence of Morris, rich colours had become subtle, and better co-ordinated. This period is considered by many to be the pinnacle of both public and domestic stained glass work.

ART DECO

Between the First and Second World Wars, shapes became more brittle and angular. Public architecture swung away from the Romantic to the Classical, and decorative glass included heroic motifs. Domestically, autumnal tints were fashionable, and the sun ray motif was used everywhere. Many will recall the galleon in full sail on the front door. Typical of the period was the pottery of Clarice Cliff, who produced colourful images of windmills, cottages and trees for her 'Bizarre' ware.

THE MODERN AGE

Domestic stained glass became irrelevant during the massive reconstruction following the Second World War. By the 1960s fashion dictated that period details should be ripped out or obscured, making way for an energetic new future in which anything seemed possible. But with the passage of time, we are becoming increasingly aware of what the past has to offer to us today. With modern technology at our fingertips, there has never been a better time to bring colour back into our lives.

Facing page: This classic window from Louis Comfort Tiffany depicts a mid-Eastern vista.

Roger Fry's Omega workshop created this decorative roundel in 1913.

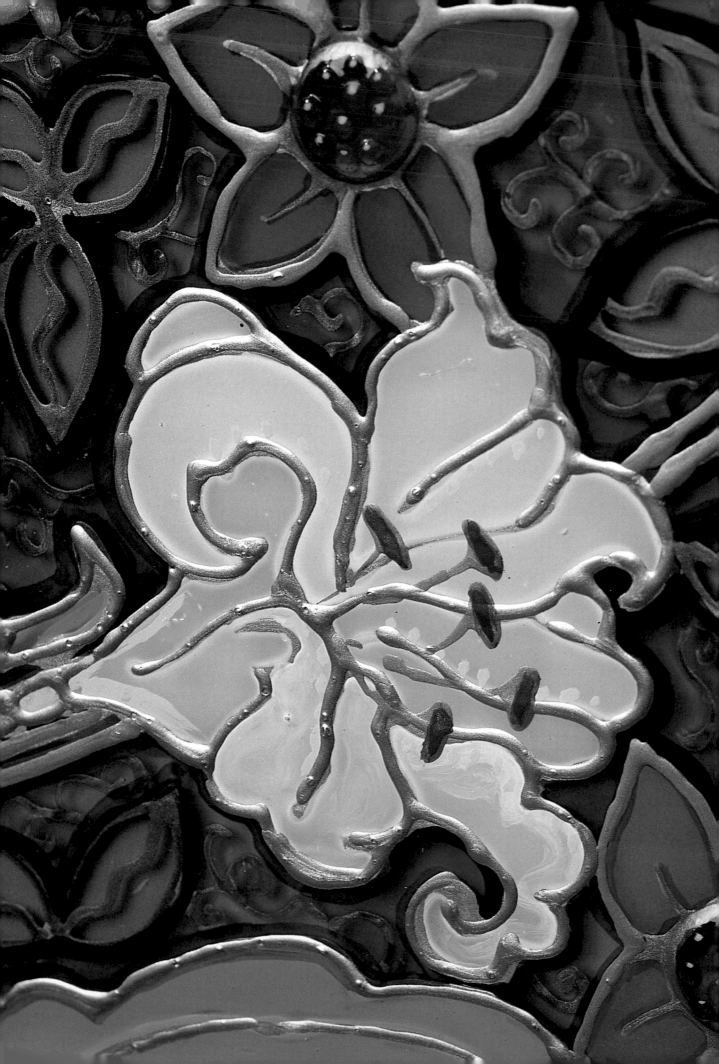

ESSENTIAL TECHNIQUES

THE PROJECTS IN THIS BOOK ENCOMPASS A WIDE RANGE OF
IDEAS AND ARE SUITABLE FOR BEGINNERS AS WELL AS THOSE
MORE EXPERIENCED IN THE CRAFT OF GLASS PAINTING.
THEY ALL RELY ON A FEW BASIC TECHNIQUES THAT ARE
FULLY DESCRIBED ON THE FOLLOWING PAGES, AND EASY TO
MASTER. PRACTISING THESE ESSENTIAL TECHNIQUES ON
SCRAPS OF GLASS, DISCARDED JAM JARS, OLD BOWLS OR
LAMPS FOUND IN JUNK SHOPS WILL IMPROVE YOUR SKILLS
AND INCREASE YOUR CONFIDENCE BEFORE TACKLING AN
IMPORTANT PIECE DESTINED FOR YOUR HOME OR AS A GIFT.

MATERIALS

Glass painting materials are available from art and craft shops and from some DIY stores. Selecting good materials can be bewildering, especially as many manufacturers use obscure names for their products. If you can, ask advice from a friend who uses glass paints already. It is helpful to have a clear idea of what you intend to do, so that you can ask specific questions. Household kitchenware, for instance, will need to withstand frequent washing, whereas a panel for a door should be lightfast. Not all materials will be suitable in both circumstances.

GLASS

Clear glass for windows is available in a range of thicknesses. Choose from many specialist treatments and finishes including a wide variety of obscured designs for window glass or mirrored glass. A good glazier can give advice on the thickness desirable for a particular location and size – usually the thickness increases with size, for safety. Glaziers will also advise on toughened or laminated glass, and fire resistance. Safety considerations are vital, especially where glass is difficult to focus on, such as in patio doors. Security is also top of the list for front doors and accessible windows.

An effective way to protect a painted window is to have it made into a double glazed unit. This is often called a 'sealed unit' and most glaziers will make one up for you. A sealed unit is thicker than a single pane, so check that your frame will accept one, or make adjustments, using wooden mouldings to support it.

PLASTIC SHEET & SECONDARY DOUBLE GLAZING

Plastic sheet is available in many forms and thicknesses. It can be quite useful as an alternative to glass in certain conditions, being lighter in weight and less breakable. All adhesive materials work perfectly with plastics, but the same cannot be said of paints. Some paints may attack certain plastics. Given the wide variety of both plastics and paints, the simplest answer is to experiment on a scrap piece first. Many forms of plastic sheet are available from garden centres and DIY stores.

Secondary double glazing is particularly useful where a large piece of glass cannot be laid flat for working on. Many systems are available and most are quite good-looking.

ACRYLIC OUTLINE PASTE

Before glass paints are applied, most designs need to be defined with a solid outline. A relief outline provides a raised border around each 'pool' of paint. Acrylic outline paste, the most commonly used medium, is squeezed straight from the tube (like icing a cake) to trace the design directly onto the glass. Mistakes are simply corrected by wiping off the paste while it is wet or scraping it off after it has dried. Misleadingly known as 'liquid lead', it contains no lead at all. It is widely available in several colours, under a variety of trade names and, as the various brands handle quite differently, you will need to experiment. Outline paste itself is not durable. Paint over it with glass paints or varnish to give it a surface that can be washed by hand.

ADHESIVE LEAD

Adhesive lead is real lead, and is weatherproof. It is produced for the double glazing industry in a variety of widths and profiles. To apply, peel off the backing strip to reveal the adhesive, and stick directly on to the glass,

burnishing firmly into place. Broader strips are mainly used in straight lines to create a cottagey lattice effect. The finer ones are used for the designs, because they bend easily around corners. Adhesive lead can be used with glass paints or adhesive coloured film. It is available from DIY stores that sell double glazing materials. Lead is poisonous, so wear lightweight household or gardening gloves, kept specifically for handling it. Wash your hands well afterwards. Do not allow children to play with it.

GLASS PAINTS

Glass paints are transparent lacquers, but each brand is different from the next. There are no established standards for glass paints, since each has been developed in isolation. Quality varies, so test for suitability before planning a major project. The main difference between paints is the solvent used: in other words, whatever is used to clean the paintbrush. This is usually white spirit or methylated spirit – check on the type of solvent used when you buy the paint. The various brands cannot be mixed with each other to make other colours, though they may be used side by side. Most paints are touch-dry in 10 minutes, but you should allow 2 days for them to harden completely.

VARNISH

Applied generously, glass paint will resist everyday knocks and moisture (but usually not a dishwasher). However, acrylic varnish or water-based polyurethane varnish are becoming more widely available. They do not affect the chemical constituents of the glass paint when hardened and as they dry by evaporation they will not yellow as oil-based varnishes do. Apply liberally with a soft brush.

COLOURED ADHESIVE FILM

This is now commonly used on front doors and conservatory windows. Double glazing companies use it because it resists fading and is weatherproof, so is far more reliable than many paints. It is available from DIY stores that stock double glazing products. The colour ranges vary from basic primaries through to remarkable 'cathedral' finishes, with two or three colours swirled across each other. After cutting to shape, the backing sheet is peeled away to reveal the adhesive, and the film is smoothed into place onto wet glass. Colours may be mixed by overlapping the sheets. Authentic stained glass designs work particularly well, but areas of film can also be used freely, without any outline. As with a painted finish, large areas should be broken down into smaller shapes.

ETCHING PASTE

This paste is applied to clear glass through a plastic stencil to produce a permanent frosted finish. Some brands contain a certain amount of hydrofluoric acid. Others are less hazardous but perhaps not as effective, and may need longer or repeated applications to work well. It may be obtained from glaziers, who use it regularly, or from large stained glass suppliers. As the finish gains popularity, it is becoming more readily available from craft suppliers.

GLASS JEWELS

A 'jewel' is any glass decoration, glued onto the surface of a pane of glass, to pinpoint light and add sparkle. It may be a glass 'glob' or 'nugget' or one of a number of fine faceted pieces made especially for use with stained glass. Many are coloured, most are clear. Wonderful 'bevel clusters' are becoming very popular for use on front doors and conservatories. Glass nuggets are readily available where candles or flower-arranging materials are sold. More striking pieces are sold by suppliers of stained glass and double glazing materials.

MIRROR GLASS

Mirror glass is most effective as a decoration when applied as a mosaic. The mosaic reflects a broken image which scatters light in all directions – it makes the perfect background to candlelight. Mirror mosaic can be embellished with glass paints, or the glass fragments can be defined using paste outliner over the grouting.

EQUIPMENT & TOOLS

It may come as a pleasant surprise that simple household tools and equipment are all you will need for many of the projects in this book. With a little experience, you will quickly get to know which specialist tools you really need.

PAINTBRUSHES

Any soft paintbrush will do for glass painting. You will need a range of sizes for delicate details and larger areas.

PENS AND PAPER

A selection of felt-tipped pens and some strong paper will help with making patterns and templates which can be fixed behind the glass for larger projects. Use a coloured ball-point pen and carbon paper to trace a design onto any surface which is not transparent, such as tiles, mirrors or coloured adhesive film.

TAPE

Use masking tape, rather than adhesive tape, to secure the design to the glass, and for other small jobs. The low tack of masking tape leaves no residue on the glass.

BONING PEG

Originally made of bone, this tool is used for burnishing adhesive lead into place. Nylon versions are available from DIY stores, but you can improvise by using a ballpoint pen with the lid on to rub down the lead.

SQUEEGEE

The type used to clean car windows will work very well. Use it to remove excess water when positioning adhesive film onto wet glass.

CHISEL, SCISSORS AND CRAFT KNIFE

You will need a small square-ended chisel for cutting off the lead neatly. The lead will cut easily, being very soft and quite thin. A pair of old scissors is useful for trimming lead, but a good sharp pair is needed to cut adhesive film. A craft knife helps with correcting mistakes in outline paste and cutting out a mask for etching.

LIGHT BOX

At the painting stage, it is essential to arrange good lighting underneath the glass. Without this, colour correction is difficult and mistakes and uneven patches will pass unseen. A light box is very effective, but expensive. See page 21 for a simple way to improvise.

CLEANING MATERIALS

Simple household methods are effective. Clean glass with a solution of washing-up liquid or a little methylated spirit, and polish with a soft, lint-free cloth. Paper towels will help with smudges and paintbrush-cleaning. Lay newspaper under the paints, so that any spills can be poured back into the paint pots.

COLOUR SCHEMING

Pure colour is the essence of glass painting. Make several copies of a design and use coloured pencils to try out variations of your colour choice. A 'colourful' window may actually have only a limited colour range, but be carefully planned. The areas allowed to remain clear will give the colours 'breathing space'.

WHERE TO START

Art classes at school will probably have given you the basics, and a visit to the library may provide inspiration, but there is nothing like simply playing with colours. Start by trying out colours on the paper template with coloured pencils. Here are some basic guidelines to help you avoid the obvious pitfalls.

THE PRIMARIES

Red, yellow and blue are colours in their purest form. They are a joyful group, recalling poppies in sunny cornfields, with a clear summer sky. Blend just a little to create richer shades for the lantern on page 38, the Tiffany-style lampshade on page 100, and the stained glass windows in the teddies' castle on page 110.

THE SECONDARIES

Purple, green and orange can be mixed from any two primaries. The secondaries are often found in subjects from nature, so start by establishing things like leaves. This will give you a framework so that you can plan other colours. Work with the background areas until you have developed a setting which shows the subject at its best, without competing with it.

Primary colours mix to give you all the other colours.

The opposites red and green are a popular combination.

OPPOSITES

On the 'colour-wheel' often used to teach colour theory, each primary has a secondary directly opposite. In their purest forms, these are very powerful colour combinations. You may want to blend the colours further to soften them. Each pair will mix to give you brown.

Red and green are a favourite pair of opposites. Find this combination in the long window and fanlight on page 50, and the Mackintosh rose used on pages 72 and 120. The powerful contrast of yellow and purple compare with the daring colours of the Clarice Cliff uplighter on page 84. The kingfisher on page 104 combines clear orange with turquoise, set against neutral colours which do not compete for attention.

THE TERTIARIES

These form an endless palette, each created from a blend of any three colours, and include shades such as peach, olive, grey-green and cream. Tertiary colours are perfect for many of the grand Edwardian designs. With a design, decide which element is the focal point and consider the background and borders Try out some colour variations to achieve a balance between the design elements, so that the eye is drawn to the focal point. The colours will benefit from blending with black or brown for an authentic feel. (See the Victorian front door on page 46.)

RELATED COLOURS

Colour mixing does not end there, of course. Endless variations are possible within just one group of

Opposites can be combined to give bold, dramatic results.

related colours. Look at the blue group alone: the peacock table lamp on page 58, the firescreen in the style of a Morris tapestry on page 68, the patio doors on page 76, the blue mirror on page 124 and the bathroom tiles on page 140. Autumn colours have long been a favourite: see the leaf design for the study-bedroom window on page 126, which falls within the yellow/orange/ green/brown group. Combine any of these with the textures of mirror or etching, with the neutrals, black and white, and you have a recipe for success.

The tertiaries combine to give gentle, mellow tones.

PAINTING GLASS

The following pages introduce the basic techniques, including an indication of drying times, which materials are weatherproof – and what to do if you make a mistake. You will also find guidance on the type of facilities required, so that you know if it will be safe to use the kitchen table or if you will need a workshop, and what to do if the glass cannot be laid flat. Clear, detailed instructions are accompanied by step-by-step photographs.

GETTING STARTED

• The glass must be scrupulously clean before you paint it: any grease or dust will spoil the finished painted surface.

• Use a soft paintbrush when painting. Squeeze it in a paper towel and clean with the solvent recommended by the manufacturer when changing colours.

• Apply the paste or lead outline before you add the glass paint. Paint quickly around the outside edge of each section. Add more paint in the centre, keeping the paint wet over the whole area. Paint right onto the outline paste to help to seal it. Finally smooth out the paint and allow it to dry naturally. Good quality paints will flatten out and brush marks will disappear.

• With the glass flat on the table, it will be impossible to judge the paint finish. Lift the glass from time to time, checking for gaps and uneven areas, or work on a light box.

• Bubbles and dust are two of the biggest enemies of glass paint. A cocktail stick or toothpick will sort out both. Use the tip of the stick to pull them towards the outline where they can be removed.

FLAT OR VERTICAL?

In an ideal world, the project should be laid flat on a table, simply because

Paint generously, so that the paint flows freely and flattens itself out. Remember to replace the lids of the jars once you have finished to prevent paint evaporation.

it is so much more accessible. The assumption is that paint will run on a vertical surface. It does, of course, but it is also less comfortable to work vertically. With the project on a table, it is much easier to apply a good generous coat of paint. If you have to work on a vertical surface, adhesive materials are the obvious answer. There is no need to double glaze, as these materials are all weatherproof.

If you do need to use paints on a vertical surface, load the brush well with paint, start at the top of a section, and when you reach the bottom wipe the excess paint off your brush back into the pot. Finish by brushing lightly downwards over the area, and allow the paint to flatten out. With the brush, wipe out any runs that form in the paint. To speed up the process, use a hair-dryer to dry a section at a time.

AN IMPROVISED LIGHT BOX

With the glass flat on the table, all glass paint colours seem much darker than they really are, and also look more even. Mistakes can easily pass unseen until it is too late to correct them. The fleur-de-lis (below) is blotchy and the paint does not fill the outline completely. A simple solution for small pieces is to lift

the glass as you paint. The light underneath will show up any mistakes before the paint dries. For bigger pieces, a light box is very helpful, but it is an expensive piece of equipment.

To improvise, you will need some white paper, a desk light and something to lift the glass off the table by about 10cm (4in), such as books or blocks of wood. Lay the white paper on the table, with the desk light shining downwards onto it. Position the blocks on the white paper so that you can support the glass on them (below). The light floods under the glass onto the white paper, making it easier to see what you are doing.

PAINTING LARGE AREAS

It can be difficult to obtain a good finish on a large area. If you paint slowly and carefully, each brush stroke has time to dry, so speed is the secret. First, use outliner to break up large areas of a single colour into a network of smaller sections, like real stained glass. Then paint all around the outside edge of each shape and fill in across the centre before the paint has had time to dry. Tidy up the painted area with one or two slow strokes and leave it. That will allow the paint to flatten itself out. Protect it from dust and any breeze.

Working with the glass flat on the table makes it more likely for mistakes to pass unseen.

Working with light underneath your work will ensure any mistakes show up before the paint dries.

CURVED SURFACES

A double curvature, like a goldfish bowl, is the most difficult surface to paint. In the first place, it will be difficult to transfer the design, because it will not lie flat against the glass. To overcome this, trim the paper template close to the edge of the design and then cut 'tucks' into it. You will start to lose parts of the design in the 'tucks' so make further adjustments until it is all workable. Before you start to paint, take time to work out how best to support the object: you may find a box helpful, or a cushion.

MIRRORS

Mirrors pose two problems. First, because mirror glass is not transparent, the design cannot be traced. Use carbon paper to transfer the design. Make sure the surface is really clean, and lay the carbon paper face down on top of the mirror. Lay the paper pattern face up on top of the carbon paper and, with a little masking tape, secure all three layers together. Use a coloured ballpoint pen to draw around the design, so that you can tell if anything has been missed.

Second, colours reflected into themselves become very dense. If you would prefer more delicate colours, mix with clear glass paint.

TILES

Tiles pose exactly the same problems as mirror, and the answers are the same. The light does not penetrate the tile, so the colours may be very heavy; again, use clear glass paint to soften the colours.

CONDENSATION

This potential enemy is only a problem if you have been unable to lay the glass flat, or choose not to use adhesive materials. With the glass flat, it is easy to give the surface a generous coat of good quality paint that will withstand the constant soaking of condensation.

Consider using secondary glazing if condensation is a likely problem – you can apply the design to secondary glass and fix it in place following the manufacturer's instructions. Use exterior quality adhesive pads to fix a unit to a metal or plastic window frame. A good glazier or DIY store will stock crystals to combat the moisture.

DOUBLE GLAZING

Once two sheets of glass are sealed together, the only accessible areas are the two outside surfaces. A design looks better if the lead is on both sides of the glass, however this is not always possible and a compromise may be necessary. If it is difficult to see the outside of a window from close up or if it is too inaccessible, you could consider working a design on the inside surface only using adhesive materials. In other cases you could introduce a design on a third piece of glass and attach that to an existing double glazed unit. A full-length fixed window alongside a front door is just the place for this approach.

If both sides of the double glazing are easily accessible, you can use a trick to deceive the eye. An overall diamond lattice, or Georgian-style squares, can be worked on the outside with flat lead, and can look quite acceptable. On the inside, add a coloured border. Try a rambling rose stem or vine in fine outline lead, with adhesive film to colour the flowers. This method is ideal for patio doors.

AFTERCARE

Tips on the aftercare of finished pieces accompany the projects that follow, as it will depend upon the individual method and materials used. As a general rule, it is better to polish rather than wash painted surfaces. Test a small area first. Doors and windows that collect condensation should be wiped with a damp cloth and allowed to dry naturally: window cleaner sprays or paste cleaners may be too harsh.

ACHIEVING COLOUR VARIATIONS

Paler colours are achieved by mixing with a clear medium from the same paint range, often called 'varnish'. Adding solvent will not make the colours paler, but simply 'thinner'. This will result in poor coverage and faster evaporation, giving an uneven finish.

Richer or stronger colours are not often successfully made by adding a second or third coat of paint. Normally this will simply dissolve the previous coat, giving an uneven finish. Good quality paints will give a rich colour with one coat. Mix colours to make darker shades. For example, try red with brown, for a brick red, or with black for a wine red.

TEXTURED PAINT FINISHES

Exciting textures can be created by stippling the paint as it dries, or drawing the paintbrush across the area slowly. Effects will vary with the drying time. A hair-dryer can be used to give a ridged surface. Painting over an area a second time will dissolve the first coat of paint, allowing you to break it up by stippling. Adding a further colour at this stage will give a marbled or water-marked effect. You can create an obscure finish in this way, so that privacy is gained without loss of light.

MARBLED PAINT FINISH

To achieve an opaque marble finish as on the chess table (see page 90) the paint was applied to the underside of the table. The veins were painted on first with a very fine paintbrush and allowed to dry. The main colours were then painted over the veins giving an opaque finish. When the glass is turned over, the top surface has the appearance of marble.

USING WHITE PAINT

In itself, white can be very heavy, almost like gloss paint, throwing all the colours out of balance. Mixed with a heavy hand, colours can look like yoghurt! However, a light touch can give exciting results. If a piece is to be seen against a dark background, add just a little white to all the colours, to make them pick up the light. See it in action in the firescreen on page 68.

CISSING

A pleasing water-mark effect in is created by cissing. Paint one area at a time and while the paint is still wet, flick a little solvent off the paintbrush onto the paint. This will attack the paint, giving the attractive appearance of fossils in marble.

Taken from Noah's Fludde (see page 6) this piece shows how striking effects can be achieved with glass paints.

PREPARING THE DESIGN

E very door and window is a different size from the next, so it is unlikely that the pattern you have fallen in love with will be exactly right for your project. Here are some simple guidelines to help you to 'fine tune' a design for your own project.

MATERIALS & EQUIPMENT

- Plain paper
- Pencil
- Felt-tipped pen, to match thickness of outline
- Straight-edge
- Photocopier
- Scissors
- Tracing paper
- Coloured pencils
- Computer (optional)

PRACTICAL TIP

Try using tracing paper to 'flip' the design, giving a mirror image, if you are decorating a pair of windows (see page 48).

ONE Start by making a template. Use strong, plain paper, such as lining paper, and draw around the window shape. To mark the centre lines to position the motif centrally, fold from top to bottom and from side to side, and mark along the creases using a felt-tipped pen.

TWO Measure out the border and draw it in, using a pen of the same thickness as the actual finished outline. The wrong thickness can give a very false impression and cause problems later.

The background grid can give a piece a very different feel.

THREE Often overlooked, the background 'grid' plays an important part in your final design. Try different ideas: it can look young, formal, cottagey or grand (see above). Perhaps this should be the first thing you decide. Full-size grids and lattice design guide sheets are available from DIY stores.

FOUR A photocopier is helpful for enlarging or copying motifs to fit the design. Cut them out and position them on the guidelines until a satisfactory layout begins to take shape. Make a tracing, then add details to this 'clean' drawing to build up the design.

FIVE Add some colour to your tracing, fix it in the window and live with it for a few days. Be prepared to make changes until you are satisfied.

SIX Since glass is transparent, you can simply trace the design directly: lay the prepared template face up on the table and position the cleaned glass over it. Tape in place with masking tape and you are ready to go. For mirrors, tiles or transparent coloured film, use carbon paper to transfer the design.

PRACTICAL TIP

It may be necessary to adapt one motif to fit several different window shapes. The ancient Tree of Life design adapts easily for a long thin window with the simple addition of several motifs and a taller urn. But the square required careful planning with a paper template. Photocopied motifs were positioned around the house name and number (see the photographs on pages 42–43).

APPLYING ACRYLIC OUTLINE PASTE

Acrylic outline paste gives a delicate outline, suitable for smaller projects or fine details within a larger window. As it is not weatherproof, outline paste is best used on an internal door, or on the inside of a window. To combat condensation, add a coat of acrylic varnish after painting. The paste dries in about 10 minutes, but you can use a hair-dryer to speed things up.

MATERIALS & EQUIPMENT

- Design template
- Glass or plastic sheet
- Masking tape
- Lint-free cloth
- Washing-up liquid
- Acrylic outline paste
- Paper towels
- Straight-edge
- Soft paintbrush
- Glass paints and solvent

PRACTICAL TIP

Mistakes are easily corrected by wiping off the paste while it is wet or scraping it off using a craft knife after it has dried.

ONE With the design template face up, position the clean glass on top and tape in place. Plan the order of working, and consider the 'route' for the lead. Any 'jewels' should be glued in place first, so that the lead can be laid down around them (see page 35). If you are working from a design in this book, position all the number 1 lead pieces first, then all the number 2 pieces and so on, so that all loose ends are secured by subsequent lengths. Make a small cut into the central groove of the lead strip and pull the two strands apart. Remove the backing strip only as the lead is laid in place, to protect the adhesive surface. Lay the strand in place, rub down with the boning peg and make a clean cut with the chisel at the end.

TWO Burnish the lead strands into place when you are satisfied with their position, using the boning peg. Take special care to rub down any points where two pieces of lead cross one another. Run the peg carefully along the full length of each piece, to ensure that it has adhered to the glass effectively. Remove the template, turn the glass over and clean well, using the lint-free cloth.

THREE Paint the design generously on the back of the glass, following the lead outline. Leave narrow gaps between the blocks of colour, and leave each colour to dry for 5 minutes before painting the adjacent one.

FOUR Allow the paint to harden for at least 3 days, before arranging the second lead outline over the painted surface. Follow the same order as for the first side, taking great care not to disturb the paint. Leave the paint to harden further before polishing the lead with lead-black for an antique finish if you wish.

C	A	U	T	I	O	N
Lead is poisonous: keep a special pair of gloves for handling it and wash your hands thoroughly afterwards.						

USING ADHESIVE LEAD & COLOURED ADHESIVE FILM

PRACTICAL TIP

You may prefer to omit the lead outline and try the design with colour only (see the Autumn Leaves on page 126 and the Mermaid Shower Screen on page 132).

This robust combination is ideal for large projects such as doors and windows as it can be applied vertically with relative ease. The lead is weatherproof and the coloured film will usually be lightfast, but should be applied on the inside of the window, where it withstands condensation well. The film is applied to wet glass. Correcting any mistakes is easy: both the film and the lead strand can simply be peeled off if you go wrong. The lead can be polished, using lead-black to give an antique finish if you wish, and the coloured film wiped over with a damp cloth.

MATERIALS & EQUIPMENT

- Carbon paper
- Coloured transparent adhesive film
- Design template
- Masking tape
- Coloured ballpoint pen
- Glass
- Scissors
- Water spray filled with dilute washing-up liquid
- Squeegee
- Twin strand adhesive lead
- Lightweight household or gardening gloves
- Small chisel
- Boning peg (or ballpoint pen with lid)
- Lint-free cloth

ONE Place the carbon paper face down over some coloured film. Position the design template over the carbon paper and tape in place. Trace the design onto the film using a coloured ballpoint pen, which makes it easier to see if you have missed a bit. Remove the design and repeat the process for each colour of film. To avoid confusion, number each piece of film on the back and cut it out only when ready to fix it in place.

TWO Tape the design in place behind the glass. Cut out the first piece of film. To apply, spray the clean glass with a weak solution of washing-up liquid. Peel the backing off the piece of film and slide it into place. It will move freely on the glass. When you are satisfied with its position carefully remove the excess water using a squeegee.

THREE Fix the remaining pieces of adhesive coloured film in position in the same way to complete the design. Allow to dry out thoroughly for at least 2 hours before applying the lead outline.

FOUR Check that there is no movement in the film pieces and work out the 'route' for the lead outline. Any 'jewels' should be glued into position at this point, so that the lead can be planned around them (see page 35). Designs in this book indicate the order of working, so that all loose lead ends are secured as the work proceeds (see page 31). Lay each strand in turn and burnish in place with the boning peg. Take particular care to rub down any points where two pieces of lead cross one another. Make sure that the lead covers the edge of the film, leaving no loose edges.

FIVE Turn the glass over and clean the reverse side thoroughly. Make the second lead outline, following the lines of the first and applying them in the same order.

C	A	U	T	I	O	N

Lead is poisonous: keep a special pair of gloves for handling it and wash your hands thoroughly afterwards.

ETCHING GLASS

This intriguing technique is excellent for giving privacy while retaining maximum daylight. It can be used anywhere, on glass of any size, inside or outside, and is a permanent finish: you can even put etched glass in the dishwasher. But etching is not something you should do on the kitchen table. Wear rubber gloves and protect the working area with polythene. You will need to have a water supply available in case of accidents and to wash off the paste when it has finished working. The time it takes will depend on the type of glass and the paste itself. To test, wash off just a little paste after waiting the recommended time. Be prepared to re-coat the test area and wait again. Mistakes cannot be corrected, so take time to prepare the masking stage carefully.

MATERIALS & EQUIPMENT

- Glass
- Washing-up liquid
- Paper towels
- Adhesive plastic stencil
- Rubber gloves
- Fitch brush or small decorator's paintbrush
- Etching paste

ONE Prepare the glass item to be etched by washing it in dilute washing-up liquid and dry thoroughly with paper towels.

TWO Mask off the areas that are to remain shiny, making a simple pattern with adhesive plastic stencils. Avoid handling the glass too much as fingermarks will slow up the etching.

THREE Wear rubber gloves to apply the paste, and work in a well ventilated area. Use a fitch brush to apply the paste covering quite thickly.

FOUR Leave for about an hour, or for the time recommended by the manufacturer, then wash off the paste with copious amounts of water. Clean the work area thoroughly and dry the glass. Remove the adhesive stencil.

APPLYING 'JEWELS'

A glass 'jewel' adds a wonderful sparkling focal point to any piece. As it is central to the design, position it first so that you can add a lead outline around it. As long as you use the correct glue to attach 'jewels', they are weatherproof and can be washed like ordinary glass. It is certainly easiest to work on a flat surface, but masking tape will help to hold the jewel on a vertical surface while the glue sets: this usually takes about 5 minutes. Mix only enough glue to do only a few 'jewels' at a time. Excess glue can be wiped away before it sets. Position 'jewels' with care, as mistakes are very difficult to correct.

MATERIALS & EQUIPMENT

- Coarse sandpaper
- Glass
- Glass 'jewels'
- Lint-free cloth
- Fast-setting two-part clear epoxy resin glue
- Scrap of card
- Toothpick
- Masking tape

ONE Using coarse sandpaper, roughen the area on the glass where the 'jewel' is to be positioned. Lay the sandpaper flat on the table and roughen the base of the 'jewel'. Clean all surfaces of dust and grease.

TWO Mix the two-part glue following the manufacturer's instructions. Squeeze a small blob of epoxy resin onto the card, and next to it a blob the same size of hardener. Use a toothpick to stir the two together thoroughly.

THREE Apply a little glue to the base of the 'jewel' and place in position on the sanded glass. Use a little masking tape to keep it in position. Fast-setting epoxy resin glue will usually harden in about 5 minutes.

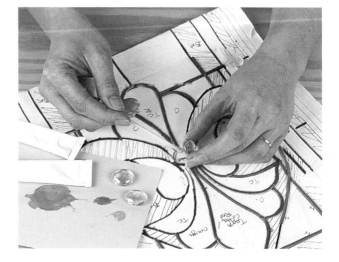

ENTRANCE
& HALLWAY

THE ENTRANCE TO YOUR HOME SAYS A GREAT DEAL ABOUT

IT AND ABOUT YOU. THE FRONT DOOR, ESPECIALLY, IS A

CHANCE FOR YOU TO PRESENT TO THE WORLD A HIGHLY

PERSONAL REFLECTION OF YOUR CHOICE OF COLOURS AND

STYLE AND EVEN A STATEMENT OF YOUR ASPIRATIONS.

VISIBLE FROM BOTH INSIDE AND OUTSIDE THE HOUSE, A

DECORATIVE GLASS DOOR PANEL MUST BE CAREFULLY

PLANNED TO CO-ORDINATE WITH AND ENHANCE BOTH.

ALLOW THE PERIOD AND STYLE OF YOUR HOME TO

INFLUENCE THE DESIGN, ALONG WITH PERSONAL

CONSIDERATIONS OF PREFERENCE AND COLOUR. IDEALLY

THE DOOR AND HALLWAY SHOULD BECOME A SINGLE

HARMONIOUS GROUP WHICH LOOKS AS THOUGH IT HAS

ALWAYS BEEN THERE.

FLEUR-DE-LIS LANTERN

What a lovely way to stamp your personality on the entrance to your home: a glowing welcome for all your visitors. Even security lights are often disguised as lanterns now, so they can also be decorated in this way. Choose a motif from the design directory that follows to reflect your own style.

TECHNIQUE FOCUS

Applying acrylic outline paste see page 26

MATERIALS & EQUIPMENT

• Lantern
• Design template
• Masking tape
• Lint-free cloth
• Washing-up liquid
• Acrylic outline paste
• Paper towels
• Craft knife
• Soft paintbrush
• Glass paints and solvent

PRACTICAL TIP

Rich colours, weather-proof finish and light fastness are achieved only by using good quality paints.

ONE If the glass in your lantern is removable, lay the design template face up and position the glass over it. If you cannot remove the glass, position the design inside the lantern, facing outwards, and ensure that the lantern is steady before you begin work. Secure the design in place with masking tape. Clean any finger-marks with a lint-free cloth and a little dilute washing-up liquid, then avoid touching the glass if possible.

TWO Pipe the paste directly from the tube. The hand you write with should guide the tip of the tube, following the design, while the other hand gently pinches the rolled end to control the flow of the paste. Remember, mistakes are easy to correct: use a paper towel to wipe away mistakes while wet, or scrape them away with a craft knife when dry. Allow the outline to dry, for about 10 minutes, then remove the paper pattern from the back.

THREE Using a soft paintbrush, paint the design with glass paint. Lift the glass from time to time, to check that the paint is even. Allow the brush onto the outline as you paint. This will not spoil the outline, and will help to seal it. This is especially important if it is not possible to remove the glass, as the decor-ation will be on the outside.

FOUR Replace the glass in the lantern with the painted side facing inwards: this will help to protect the decoration from the weather.

FLEUR-DE-LIS

HAPPY SUN

HAPPY MOON AND STARS

TRADITIONAL ROSE

PORCH WINDOW

This small, awkward window, right beside the front door, gave a view straight into the house. The ancient Tree of Life design was adapted to frame the house name and number, giving a dense overall texture to provide much-needed privacy. As much as the front door itself, the decoration around it helps to set the tone for the entrance, so plan both together carefully.

MATERIALS & EQUIPMENT

- Design template
- Masking tape
- Coarse sandpaper
- Glass 'jewels'
- Fast-setting two-part clear epoxy resin glue
- Toothpick
- Scrap of card
- Lightweight household or gardening gloves
- Twin strand adhesive lead
- Small chisel
- Boning peg (or ballpoint pen with lid)
- Acrylic outline paste (black and gold)
- Paper towels
- Craft knife
- Soft paintbrush
- Glass paints and solvent

TECHNIQUE FOCUS

Preparing the design
see page 24

Using lead outline with
paste on back see page 28

Applying 'jewels'
see page 35

ONE With the design template face up, position the clean glass on top and tape in place.

TWO Apply the 'jewels' first. Using coarse sandpaper, roughen the areas of glass where they are to be positioned, and the bases of the 'jewels'. Clean all surfaces. Mix the two-part glue following the manufacturer's instructions. Use a toothpick to apply a little glue to the base of a 'jewel' and place in position on the prepared glass. Use masking tape to hold it in position. Fast-setting epoxy resin glue will usually harden in about 5 minutes. Repeat for all the 'jewels'.

THREE Consider the 'route' for the lead outline. Wearing gloves to protect your hands, add the lead strips following the sequence of numbers given on the design, so that all loose ends are secured as the work proceeds.

FOUR Burnish the lead when you are satisfied with its position, using the boning peg. Take special care to rub down any points where two pieces of lead cross one another. Run the peg carefully along the full length of each piece, to ensure that it has adhered to the glass effectively. Remove the paper template.

FIVE Turn the glass over, using cushions to protect the 'jewels', and clean well. Using acrylic outline paste, follow the lead outline. Allow to dry (about 10 minutes).

SIX Add the house name and number using gold outline paste, so that they can easily be seen from a distance. Allow to dry.

SEVEN Paint the design with a soft brush, lifting the glass frequently to check that the paint is even. Allow the brush onto the outline as you paint to help to seal it.

PRACTICAL TIP

If you add the house name and number to the inside of the window, remember to reverse it!

DESIGN DIRECTORY

NUMBERS INDICATE THE ORDER
OF WORKING WITH LEAD OUTLINE

TREE OF LIFE

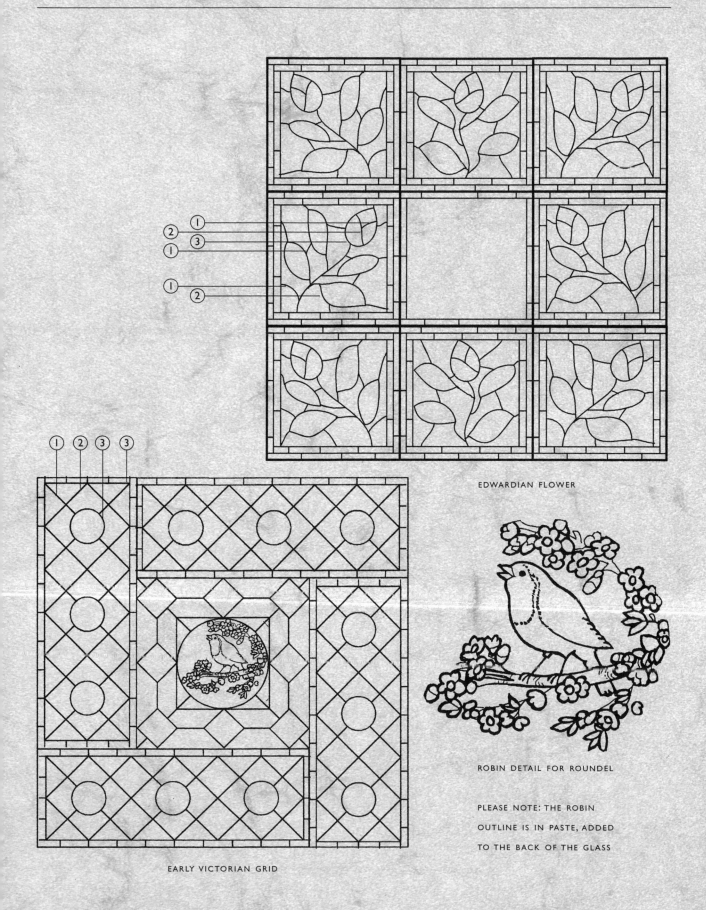

EDWARDIAN FLOWER

EARLY VICTORIAN GRID

ROBIN DETAIL FOR ROUNDEL

PLEASE NOTE: THE ROBIN
OUTLINE IS IN PASTE, ADDED
TO THE BACK OF THE GLASS

VICTORIAN FRONT DOOR

This elaborate front door was painstakingly planned to blend with a remarkable mosaic tiled floor. Though restricted to terracotta, black and white, the tiles create a dazzling effect. Used with holly green, the muted colours of the painted glass panels rely on textures for interest, so as to avoid competing with the mosaic. The original door was renovated, with 1950s modifications stripped away. Design elements such as the gothic arch and the tile motif at the base of the panel reflect the features and period style of the house, to enhance the entire entrance and hallway.

MATERIALS & EQUIPMENT

• Paper and pencil
• Felt-tipped pen
• Coloured pencils
• Masking tape
• Coarse sandpaper
• Glass 'jewels'
• Lint-free cloth
• Fast-setting two-part clear epoxy resin glue
• Toothpick
• Scrap of card
• Lightweight household or gardening gloves
• Twin strand adhesive lead
• Old scissors
• Small chisel
• Boning peg (or ballpoint pen with lid)
• Cushions
• Glass paints and solvent
• Soft paintbrush
• Paper towels
• Lead-black (optional)

ONE Make a paper template of the windows and adapt the design to fit as necessary. Colour the paper pattern with coloured pencils to find a colour scheme you like. With the design template face up, position the clean glass on top and tape in place.

TWO Plan the sequence of work and consider the 'route' for the lead. The 'jewels' should be glued in place at the start, so that the lead can be laid around them. Using coarse sandpaper, roughen the areas of glass where they are to be positioned, and the bases of the 'jewels'. Clean all surfaces. Mix the two-part glue following the manufacturer's instructions. Use a toothpick to apply a little glue to the base of a 'jewel' and place in position on the prepared glass. Use masking tape to keep it in position. Fast-setting epoxy resin glue will usually harden in about 5 minutes. Repeat for all the 'jewels'.

THREE Wearing gloves to protect your hands, add the lead, following the sequence of numbers on the design, so that all loose ends are secured as the work proceeds.

TECHNIQUE FOCUS

Preparing the design
see page 24

Applying lead outline back and front see page 30

Applying 'jewels'
see page 35

FOUR Burnish the lead when you are satisfied with its position, using the boning peg. Take special care to rub down any points where two pieces of lead cross one another. Run the peg carefully along the full length of each piece, to ensure that it has adhered to the glass effectively.

FIVE Remove the paper template. Using cushions to protect the 'jewels', turn the glass over and clean well.

SIX Paint the design generously on the back of the glass, following the outline on the front. Leave narrow gaps between the blocks of colour, and allow each colour to dry before painting the adjacent one.

SEVEN Allow the paint to harden for at least 3 days, before applying the lead outline over the painted surface. Follow the same order as for the first side, taking great care not to disturb the paint.

EIGHT Allow to harden further before polishing the lead with lead-black for an antique finish if you wish.

DESIGN DIRECTORY

NUMBERS INDICATE THE ORDER OF WORKING WITH LEAD OUTLINE

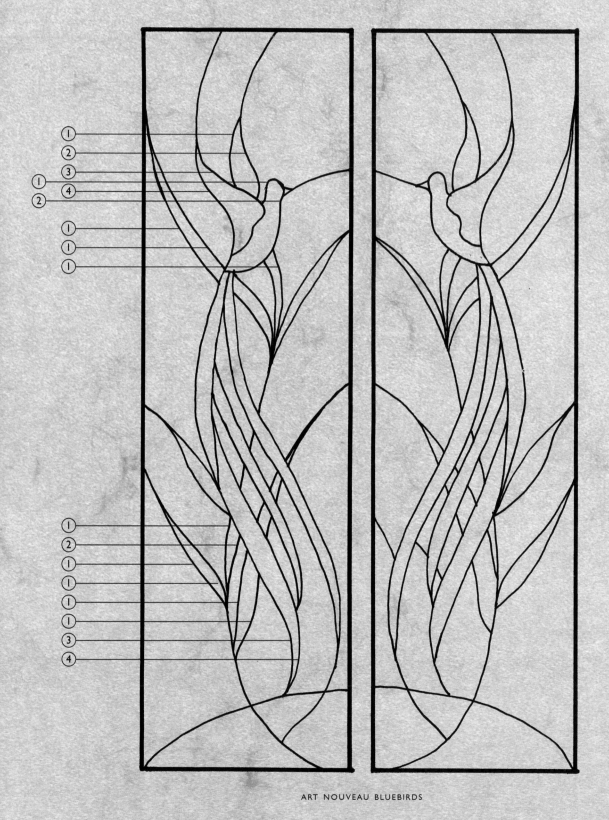

ART NOUVEAU BLUEBIRDS

EDWARDIAN LILIES

CLASSIC VICTORIAN PANEL

ROSE TRELLIS WINDOW

Not all windows are simple to decorate. this one is typical of many modern houses. The plain windows are already double glazed, and certainly cannot be laid flat. This particular window also has a Georgian-style grid in lead, and textured, obscured glass on the inside of the glazed unit. One solution would be to triple-glaze the windows, adding an extra piece of glass to the existing frame, with wooden moulding to hold it in place. Fixed to the inside of the window, it should give no trouble with condensation. An alternative is to use adhesive film rather than paint with the lead. As film needs a really flat surface, both lead and film have been applied to the outside of the window. The rose design used here to weave around the existing grid, was also used on a fanlight above the door and will adapt to many styles and shapes of window.

TECHNIQUE FOCUS

Adhesive lead and coloured adhesive film see *page 32*

MATERIALS & EQUIPMENT

- Carbon paper
- Coloured transparent adhesive film
- Design template
- Masking tape
- Coloured ballpoint pen
- Scissors
- Water spray with dilute washing-up liquid
- Squeegee
- Lightweight household or gardening gloves
- Twin strand adhesive lead
- Old scissors
- Small chisel
- Boning peg (or ballpoint pen with lid)

ONE Place a sheet of carbon paper face down over the coloured film. Position the design template over the carbon paper and tape in place. Use the coloured ballpoint pen to trace the design onto the film. Remove the design and repeat the process for each colour film. To avoid confusion, number the leaves and roses, cutting out each piece of film only when you are ready to fix it in place.

TWO Tape the paper design to the inside of the window, facing outwards.

THREE Cut out the first piece of film. To apply, spray the clean glass with a weak solution of washing-up liquid. Peel the backing off the piece of film and slide it into place. It will move freely on the glass. When you are satisfied with the position, carefully remove excess water with the squeegee. Complete the rest of the design in the same way and allow to dry out thoroughly (about 2 hours).

FOUR Check that there is no movement in the film pieces and work out the 'route' for the lead outline. Wearing gloves to protect your hands, separate the strands of the lead by making a small cut into the end with the chisel and pulling them apart. Apply the strips following the sequence of numbers given on the design, so that all loose lead ends are secured as the work proceeds. Make sure that the lead covers the edge of the film, leaving no loose edges.

FIVE Burnish the lead when you are satisfied with its position, using the boning peg. Take special care to rub down any points where two pieces of lead cross one another. Run the peg carefully along the full length of each piece, to ensure that it has adhered to the glass effectively.

DESIGN DIRECTORY

NUMBERS INDICATE THE ORDER OF WORKING WITH LEAD OUTLINE

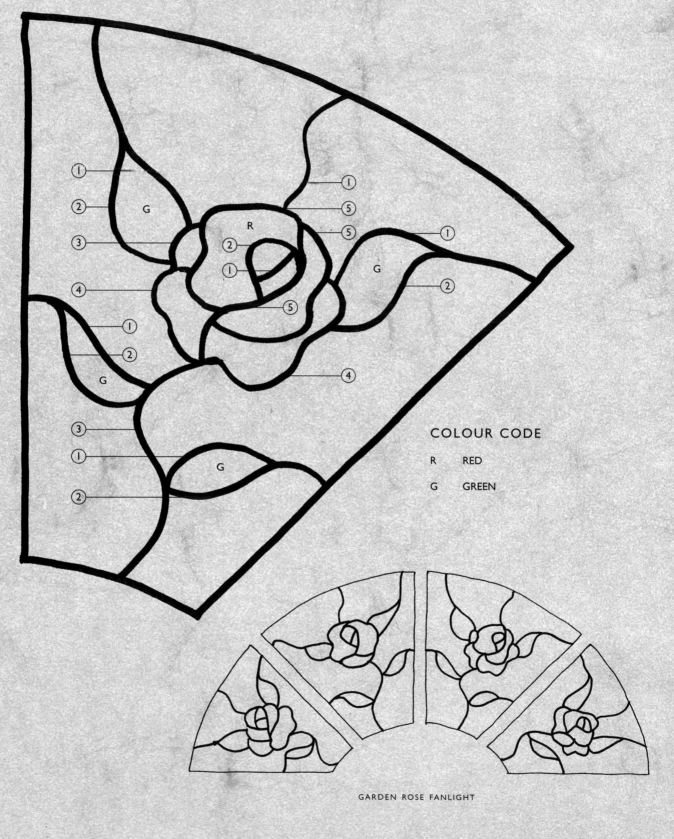

COLOUR CODE

R   RED

G   GREEN

GARDEN ROSE FANLIGHT

GARDEN ROSE PANEL

ART DECO HEARTS

UPPER PANEL

LOWER PANEL

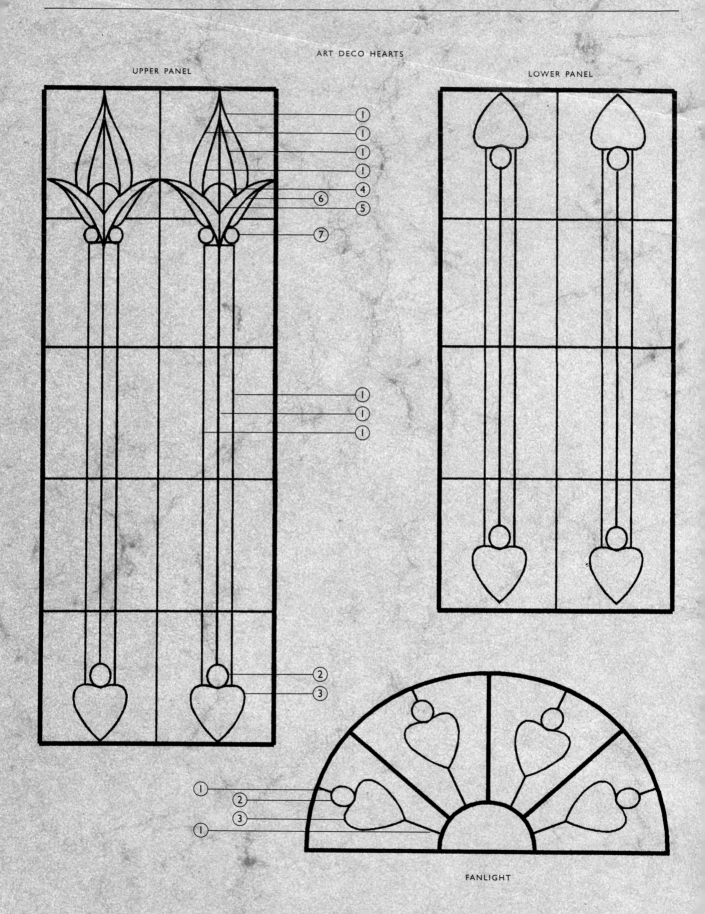

FANLIGHT

SCALLOP

UPPER PANEL

LOWER PANEL

FANLIGHT

LIVING ROOM & CONSERVATORY

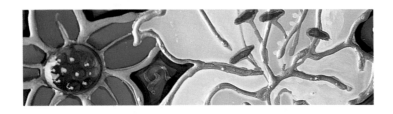

WITH INTEREST IN THE GARDEN INCREASING ALL THE TIME, WHY NOT FRAME YOUR GARDEN VIEW WITH A VINE OR CLIMBING PLANT? CARRY THE GARDEN THEME INTO THE HOUSE ITSELF, WITH THE LILY DESIGN TO LINK THE DECOR BETWEEN DINING AND SITTING ROOM OR TIE YOUR COLOURS AND STYLE INTO A FOCAL POINT, SUCH AS THE MORRIS-STYLE FIRESCREEN OR JEWEL-RICH PEACOCK TABLE LAMP. THE EVER-POPULAR DECO MOTIFS EMERGE IN A QUARTERLIGHT FOR THE THIRTIES BAY WINDOW AND THE SOPHISTICATED CLOCK AND AN UPLIGHTER IN THE EXUBERANT STYLE OF CLARICE CLIFF. THERE ARE SO MANY OPTIONS, WITH THE CHOICE OF DESIGNS TOO, YOUR LIVING AREAS WILL BE TRANSFORMED!

PEACOCK TABLE LAMP

Glowing colours in the style of Tiffany make this lamp a focal point for any room. A range of bronze-finished bases is available from stained glass suppliers, complete with electrical fittings to take a light bulb. This peacock design will adapt to fit various bases, and the design directory allows you to choose the size and style to suit your own personal taste. Although the clarity of glass paints is usually one of their most desirable qualities, in this case opaque colours will hide the light bulb when the finished lamp is in use: to make colours opaque, mix in a small amount of white glass paint.

MATERIALS & EQUIPMENT

- Fan base and glass oval
- Washing-up liquid
- Lint-free cloth
- Design template
- Masking tape
- Lightweight household or gardening gloves
- Twin strand adhesive lead
- Old scissors
- Small chisel
- Boning peg (or ballpoint pen with lid)
- Flat strip adhesive lead
- Glass jewels
- Clear epoxy resin glue
- Scrap of card
- Cocktail stick
- Acrylic outline paste in black and silver or gold
- Paper towels
- Coloured pencils
- Soft paintbrush
- Glass paints and solvent
- Old soft shoe brush
- Lead-black
- Dry cloth

ONE Clean the glass well with a little dilute washing-up liquid and dry with a lint-free cloth. With the design template face up on the table, position the glass over it and tape it in place.

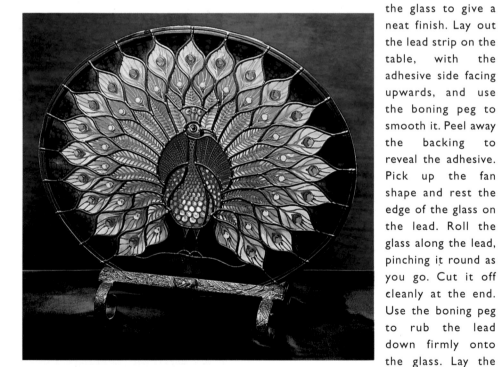

TWO Consider the 'route' the lead strand will take. The design is numbered in order of working: start at the lower edges of the peacock tail, working up to the centre top. The outline of the bird itself is used to seal all the loose ends. Wear gloves to protect your hands when working with lead. Rub down carefully with a boning peg, paying particular attention to any points where one strand crosses another. Complete the lead outline and remove the paper template.

THREE Using the flat strip lead, edge the glass to give a neat finish. Lay out the lead strip on the table, with the adhesive side facing upwards, and use the boning peg to smooth it. Peel away the backing to reveal the adhesive. Pick up the fan shape and rest the edge of the glass on the lead. Roll the glass along the lead, pinching it round as you go. Cut it off cleanly at the end. Use the boning peg to rub the lead down firmly onto the glass. Lay the glass flat on the table with the leaded design face upwards. Lay a second flat lead strip to cover both the loose ends of the design and the folded lead edge. Follow round the edge of the glass shape, and use the boning peg to rub down carefully, paying special attention to any points where the flat lead crosses a lead strand.

FOUR Add small jewels to the design if desired (see page 35).

FIVE Turn the glass over and clean the back well. Use the black outline paste to repeat the outline of the peacock on the back of the glass, following the lead outline on the front. Use both hands to guide the tube, making the paste outline the same thickness as the lead outline. Leave for 10 minutes to dry.

SIX Use the gold or silver outliner to add as much (or as little) fine detail as you choose on feathers and wings. Allow to dry thoroughly.

SEVEN Try out colour schemes with coloured pencils on the paper template. When you are satisfied, use a soft paintbrush to apply glass paint. Allow the paint to cover the edges of the outlines, both black and gold or silver, so that the paste is sealed well. Leave to harden for at least 2 days.

EIGHT With an old soft shoe brush, apply a little lead-black to the front surface. Using a circular motion, rub the polish gently into the lead design, making sure that it gets right into the corners. Polish off with a dry cloth, giving a dark glow to the lead outline. Prepare the base and fit the glass in place.

TECHNIQUE FOCUS

Using lead outline with paste on back *see page 28*

Applying 'jewels' *see page 35*

PRACTICAL TIP

Try using a wooden plate stand as support for the decorated glass of this project.

DESIGN DIRECTORY

NUMBERS INDICATE THE ORDER OF WORKING WITH LEAD OUTLINE

THIS TEMPLATE IS FOR THE
LEAD OUTLINE ON THE
FRONT OF THE GLASS

PEACOCK LEAD OUTLINE

THE FINE
BACKGROUND DETAIL
WAS MADE IN GOLD
AND SILVER OUTLINE
PASTE APPLIED TO THE
BACK OF THE GLASS

PEACOCK BACKGROUND DETAILS

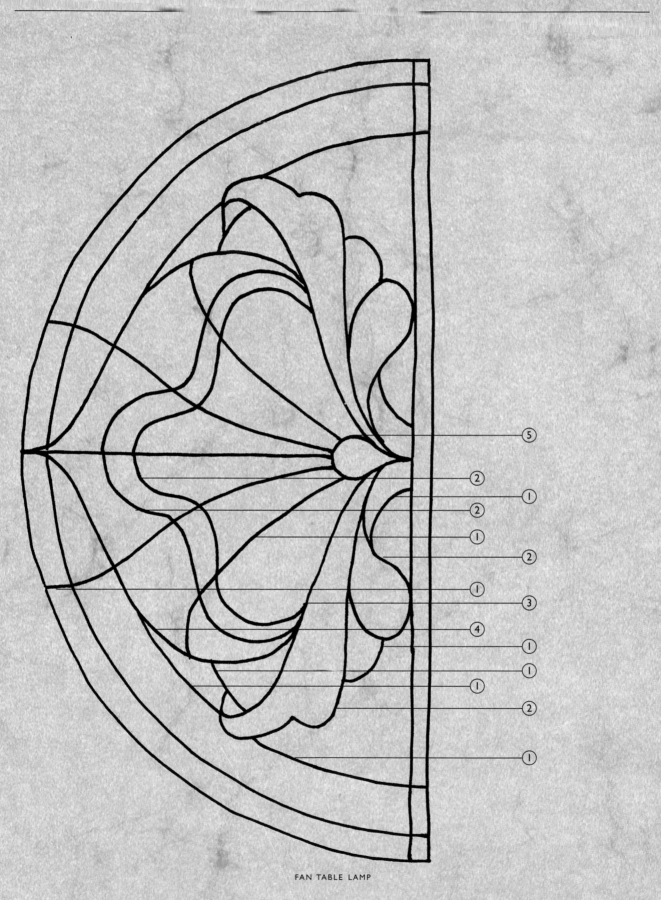

FAN TABLE LAMP

THE FOREGROUND OF THIS JAPANESE INSPIRED IRIS DESIGN IS WORKED IN LEAD.

THE BACKGROUND IS IN OUTLINE PASTE

JAPANESE IRIS

WILLIAM MORRIS FIRESCREEN

Based on the beautiful Arts and Crafts tapestries of William Morris, this firescreen will cheer your empty hearth throughout the summer months. A fireplace in summer is simply a black hole, but this sparkling design brings it to life in the daytime, and in the evening a small light in the grate will create an exciting focal point. Scour antique shops and boot fairs to find a suitable frame, or speak to a picture framer. This setting, because it has a dark background, presents a challenge for the glass painter. You can overcome it simply by painting on mirror, or mixing a little white paint to make the colours stand out. Metallic outline paste and glass 'jewels' add textural interest and catch the light, glowing against the dark background. Experiment with lighting on the front to enhance the silver and gold surface texture. A low wattage lamp behind will make the colours glow and the jewels sparkle.

MATERIALS & EQUIPMENT

- Design template
- Glass or plastic sheet
- Masking tape
- Coarse sandpaper
- Glass 'jewels'
- Fast-setting two-part clear epoxy resin glue
- Toothpick
- Scrap of card
- Acrylic outline paste in black, silver and gold
- Paper towels
- Craft knife
- Glass paints and solvent
- Soft paintbrush

PRACTICAL TIP

We used more glue to add tiny blobs with a cocktail stick to the tops of the 'jewels' to give an additional light-catching texture.

ONE Lay the template face up and position the clean glass over it. Tape in place with masking tape.

TWO With the coarse sandpaper, roughen the bases of the 'jewels' and the areas where they will be positioned. Following the manufacturer's instructions, apply a little epoxy resin glue to the

TECHNIQUE FOCUS

Applying acrylic outline paste see page 26

Applying 'jewels' see page 35

Using white paint see page 23

base of each 'jewel' and stick them in place. Secure with masking tape until the glue has hardened (about 5 minutes).

THREE With the black outline paste, follow the lines of the main design, piping directly from the tube. Allow to dry and remove the template from the back.

FOUR For the background curls, use silver paste and allow to dry thoroughly. Overpaint these background details in blue glass paint. They will glint out of the panel with a delightful metallic glow.

FIVE For the main design, mix a very little white glass paint into the colours, to make them stand out against the background. Using a soft paintbrush, paint the design generously. Allow the brush onto the outline as you paint. This will help to seal the outline, making it hand-washable. Allow to dry.

SIX Complete the panel with silver paste, going over the black outline and adding details to enliven the surface texture.

WILLIAM MORRIS STYLE TAPESTRY

JUNGLE PARROT

ART DECO SUNSET

QUARTERLIGHTS FOR A BAY WINDOW OR CONSERVATORY

In the typical bay windows of 1930s houses, the quarterlights – the row of small opening windows at the top - were each invariably decorated with a small central motif. These opening quarterlights now feature at the top of many conservatory windows. Along with the increasing popularity of conservatories, there has been a recent revival of interest in characteristic Art Nouveau and Art Deco motifs. This design features the well-loved rose motif of Charles Rennie Mackintosh. As quarterlights are often above eye level, access to the glass may be too awkward to consider using paints. Adhesive film and lead have been used on the inside of the glass. When used with adhesive film, 'jewels' should be applied after the film. This allows you to use the squeegee to remove water from the film. The lead outline is the final stage.

MATERIALS & EQUIPMENT

- Carbon paper
- Coloured transparent adhesive film
- Design template
- Masking tape
- Coloured ballpoint pen
- Scissors
- Water spray with dilute washing-up liquid
- Squeegee
- Glass 'jewels'
- Coarse sandpaper
- Fast-setting two-part clear epoxy resin glue
- Toothpick
- Scrap of card
- Lightweight household or gardening gloves
- Twin strand adhesive lead
- Old scissors
- Small chisel
- Boning peg (or ballpoint pen with lid)

ONE Place a sheet of carbon paper face down over the coloured film. Position the design template over the carbon paper and tape in place. Use a coloured ballpoint pen to trace the design onto the film. Remove the template and repeat the process for each colour film. To avoid confusion, number each piece and cut out only when you are ready to fix it in place.

TWO Tape the design template in place behind the glass.

THREE Cut out the first piece of film. To apply, spray the clean glass with a weak solution of washing-up liquid. Peel the backing off the piece of film and slide it into place. It will move freely on the glass. When you are satisfied with the position, carefully remove excess water with the squeegee. Complete the rest of the design in the same way and allow to dry out thoroughly (about 2 hours).

FOUR Next, secure any 'jewels' in the design. Using coarse sandpaper, roughen the areas where 'jewels' are to be positioned and also the base of the

'jewels'. Following the manufacturer's instructions, apply a little epoxy resin glue to the base of each 'jewel' and stick it in place. Secure with masking tape until the glue has hardened (about 5 minutes).

FIVE Check that there is no movement in the film pieces and work out the 'route' for the lead outline. Wearing gloves to protect your hands, separate the strands of the lead by making a small cut into the end with the chisel and pulling them apart. Apply the lead strips following the sequence of numbers given on the design, so that all loose lead ends are secured as the work proceeds. Make sure that the lead covers the edge of the film, leaving no loose edges.

SIX Burnish the lead when you are satisfied with its position, using the boning peg. Take special care to rub down any points where two pieces of lead cross one another. Run the peg carefully along the full length of each piece, to ensure that it has adhered to the glass effectively. Remove the paper template.

SEVEN If it is possible to gain access to the other side of the glass, make the second lead outline, following the first.

TECHNIQUE FOCUS

Preparing a design
see page 24

Adhesive lead with coloured adhesive film
see page 32

Applying 'jewels'
see page 35

DESIGN DIRECTORY

NUMBERS INDICATE THE ORDER OF WORKING WITH LEAD OUTLINE

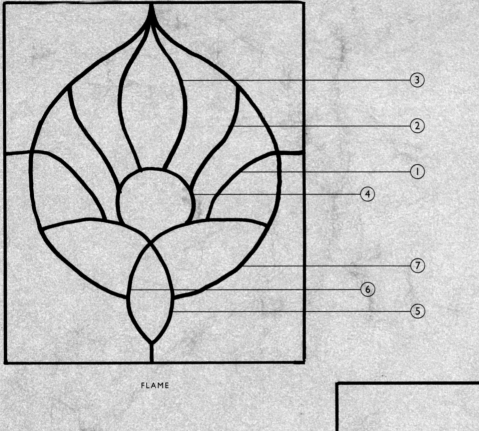

FLAME

DECO

MACKINTOSH ROSE

CLEMATIS-FRAMED PATIO DOORS

Patio doors are an essential part of many homes now, flooding the room with daylight and linking the house and garden spaces. In this clematis design, we have borrowed from the ideas and style of Louis Comfort Tiffany, drawing inspiration from the garden outside. A particular benefit of this decorative design is that it makes large glass doors safer: it not only adds to your pleasure, framing the view of the garden, but it draws attention to the glass door so that no one will walk into it by mistake! Usually such a door is already a double glazed unit and there is no question of it being laid flat, so adhesive materials are ideal. This design was applied to the inside of the window.

TECHNIQUE FOCUS

Adhesive lead outline with coloured adhesive film
see page 32

MATERIALS & EQUIPMENT

- Carbon paper
- Coloured transparent adhesive film
- Design template
- Masking tape
- Coloured ballpoint pen
- Scissors
- Water spray with dilute washing-up liquid
- Squeegee
- Lightweight household or gardening gloves
- Twin strand adhesive lead
- Small chisel
- Boning peg (or ballpoint pen with lid)

ONE Place a sheet of carbon paper face down over the coloured film. Position the design template over the carbon paper and tape in place. Use a coloured ballpoint pen to trace the design onto the film. Remove the design and repeat the process for each colour film. To avoid confusion, number each piece and cut out only when you are ready to fix it in place.

TWO Tape the design template in place on the outside of the glass, facing into the room.

THREE Cut out the first piece of film. To apply, spray the clean glass with a weak solution of washing-up liquid. Peel the backing off the piece of film and slide it into place. It will move freely on the glass. When you are satisfied with the position, carefully remove excess water with the squeegee. Complete the rest of the design in the same way and allow to dry out thoroughly – about 2 hours.

FOUR Check that there is no movement in the film pieces. Wearing gloves to protect your hands, separate the strands of the lead by making a small cut into the end with the chisel and pulling them apart. As a general guide to the order of working, do the stems first, then the leaves and finally the flowers. Remember to plan your route so that you secure all loose lead ends as the work proceeds. Make sure that the lead covers the edge of the film, leaving no loose edges.

FIVE Burnish the lead when you are satisfied with its position, using the boning peg. Take special care to rub down any points where two pieces of lead cross one another. Run the peg carefully along the full length of each piece, to ensure that it has adhered to the glass effectively. Remove the paper template.

DESIGN DIRECTORY

NUMBERS INDICATE THE ORDER OF WORKING WITH LEAD OUTLINE

1

LIFT AND TUCK UNDER

2

3

4

LIFT AND TUCK UNDER

LIFT AND TUCK UNDER

1

2

3

4

VARY THE ANGLE OF THESE SIMPLE BUTTERFLIES ON
THE WINDOW TO BRING THEM TO LIFE

BAMBOO   BUTTERFLIES

THE COMPLEX CLEMATIS AND BAMBOO SHOULD BE ENLARGED
TO FIT YOUR WINDOW. AS A GENERAL GUIDE, START WITH
THE STEMS, THEN THE LEAVES AND FINALLY THE FLOWERS

CLEMATIS

ART DECO CLOCK

Using a decorative theme to reflect your own tastes, this clock offers an exciting way to use glass paint and adhesive lead on mirror. With very minor changes, this project would be at home anywhere, and it is much easier than you would expect. Ask a local glazier to cut the glass and drill the central hole for you.

TECHNIQUE FOCUS

Textured paint finishes; mirrors see page 22

MATERIALS & EQUIPMENT

- Rectangular mirror with central hole
- Lint-free cloth
- Carbon paper
- Design template
- Masking tape
- Coloured ballpoint pen
- Soft paintbrush
- Glass paints and solvent
- Paper towels
- Lightweight household or gardening gloves
- Twin strand adhesive lead
- Old scissors
- Small chisel
- Boning peg (or ballpoint pen with lid)
- Lead-black (optional)
- Clock movement and hands

ONE Clean the mirror and position a sheet of carbon paper over it, with the design template face up on top. Tape in place.

TWO Use a coloured ballpoint pen to trace the design onto the mirror. Check that the whole design is transferred and remove the paper template and carbon paper.

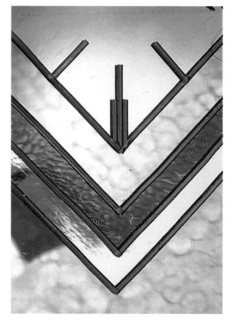

THREE Use a soft paintbrush to paint the design. Paint one large area at a time, and leave a narrow gap between areas of colour. Allow each colour to dry for 5 minutes before painting the adjacent one. The paint should be left to harden for at least 3 days before the lead outline is added over the top.

FOUR Plan the order of working, and consider the 'route' for the lead. Wearing gloves to protect your hands, separate the strands of the lead by making a small cut into the end with the chisel and pulling them apart. Apply the strips following the sequence of numbers given on the design, so that all loose lead ends are secured as the work proceeds.

FIVE Burnish the lead when you are satisfied with its position, using the boning peg. Take special care to rub down any points where two pieces of lead cross one another. Run the peg carefully along the full length of each piece, to ensure that it has adhered to the glass effectively. Remove the paper template.

SIX Allow adhesive lead to harden further before polishing the lead with lead-black to give an antique finish if desired. Attach the clock movement and hands. Most battery-run clock movements have push on hands and a threaded unit to push through the mirror and are fixed at the back with a threaded nut.

PRACTICAL TIP

Battery operated clock movements and hands are available from good craft suppliers. Take the clock movement to the glazier when you order the glass – this will enable him to cut the right sized hole for the thickness of the mirror.

DESIGN DIRECTORY

NUMBERS INDICATE THE ORDER OF WORKING WITH LEAD OUTLINE

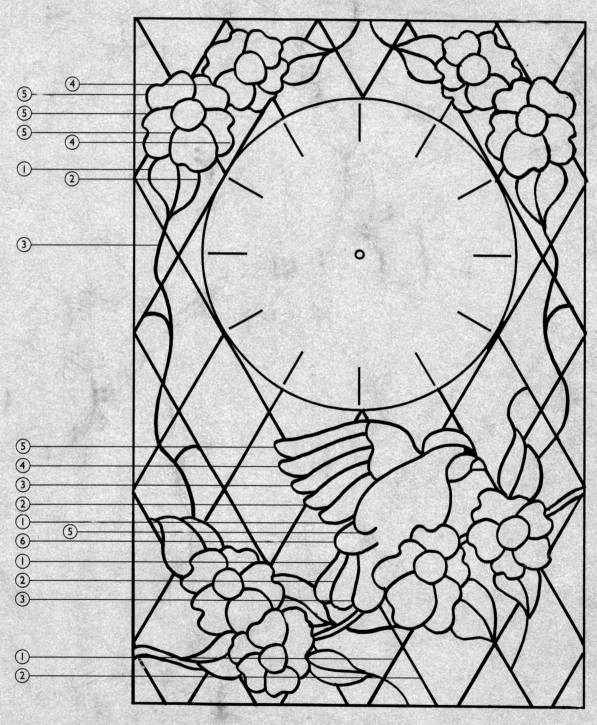

COTTAGE GARDEN CLOCK

ART DECO CLOCK

SUNRAY CLOCK

CLARICE CLIFF STYLE UPLIGHTER

This simple uplighter is decorated with details in the style of Clarice Cliff, to tie in with an Art Deco scheme. Choose your colour scheme carefully to match the decor. The Clarice Cliff design shown here is a good example of the use of secondary colours (*see page 19*). Repeat the motif on hand embroidered satin cushions, a table runner or a set of mats for the dressing table. We even had fun creating our own 'original' handpainted plate to complete the theme. This fairly standard light-fitting came from a boot sale: you will need to adapt the design if your uplighter is a different shape. You could also try this design on one of the many parchment lampshades that are widely available.

TECHNIQUE FOCUS

Preparing the design
see *page 24*

Applying acrylic outline
paste see *page 26*

MATERIALS & EQUIPMENT

- Glass light-fitting
- Washing-up liquid
- Lint-free cloth
- Tracing paper and pencil
- Felt-tipped pen
- Masking tape
- Carbon paper
- Coloured ballpoint pen
- Acrylic outline paste
- Paper towels
- Craft knife
- Soft paintbrush
- Glass paints and solvent

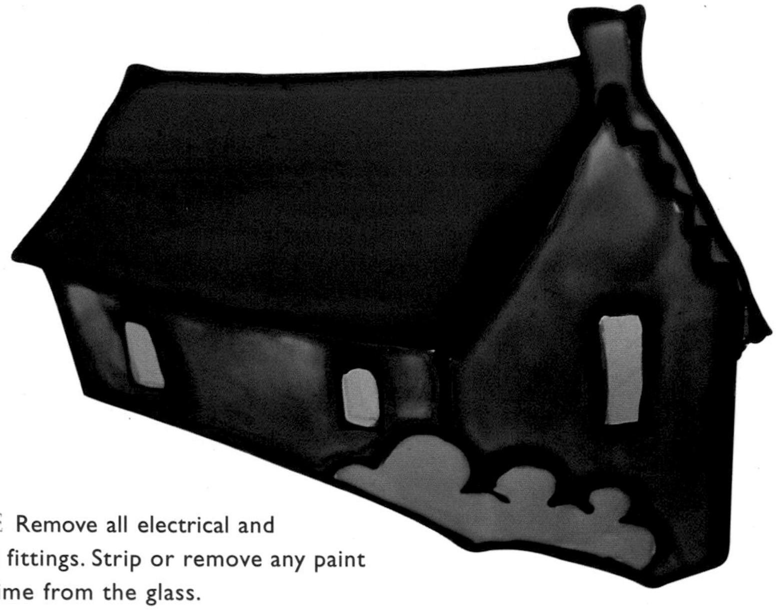

ONE Remove all electrical and metal fittings. Strip or remove any paint or grime from the glass.

TWO Prepare the design. In this instance it is easier to make a template of the light fitting. For the cherub or ribbons you might choose to use a gold or silver outline paste. Centre the designs on the template.

THREE Clean the light-fitting with dilute washing-up liquid, dry thoroughly, and then avoid touching the glass if possible. Trace the design and try it in position on the light-fitting. Adapt it to fit as necessary and position face up over the fitting. Tape in place with masking tape. Slide a sheet of carbon paper under the paper template, with the carbon side downwards. Trace the design using a ballpoint pen. Remove the template and carbon paper.

FOUR Trace the carbon outline with the paste, piping it directly from the tube. Leave to dry for about 10 minutes.

FIVE Using a soft brush, paint the design generously with glass paint. When working on a curved surface, paint on a small area and allow to dry before turning the lamp to paint the next area. Allow the paintbrush onto the outline, as you paint. This will help to seal the outline, making it hand-washable. It will not spoil the black outline.

SIX Allow to harden thoroughly, then reassemble the lamp fitting, rewiring if necessary. Use a low-wattage soft-glow light bulb.

PRACTICAL TIP

Before you start, work out how to support the light–fitting so that you have both hands free. Support the light-fitting over a light source as you paint, to give an accurate idea of how the colours on the finished fitting will look.

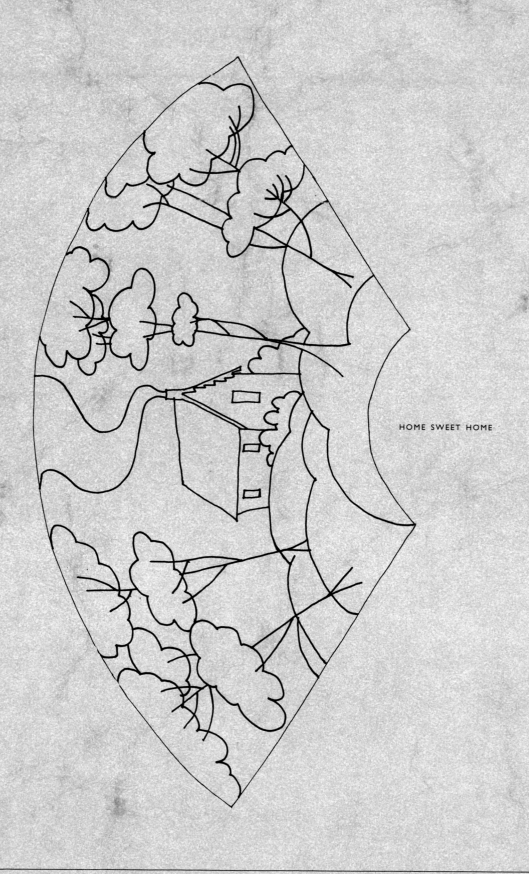

HOME SWEET HOME

CHERUBS

GEORGIAN RIBBON BOW

KITCHEN & DINING ROOM

EXTEND YOUR CREATIVE TOUCH TO THE AREAS WHERE THE FAMILY EATS TOGETHER TOO. RESCUE A POOR OUTLOOK WITH OUR KINGFISHER AND DRAGONFLIES. TRY ADDING SOME CHERRIES TO YOUR GLASS-FRONTED CUPBOARD DOORS, OR CHEER UP SOME PLAIN GLASSES WITH A STARS AND STRIPES ETCHED MOTIF. FOR A FORMAL DINING ROOM, CREATE A FOCAL POINT WITH A PENDANT LAMP IN A STYLE AND COLOURS TO ECHO YOUR FAVOURITE CUSHIONS. BUT WHY NOT DECORATE THE TABLE ITSELF? MOTIVATE THE FAMILY WITH A CHESS TABLE — THE DESIGN IS ON THE UNDERSIDE, SO IT IS PROTECTED, WITH THE TOP SIMPLY WIPED CLEAN AFTER MEALS, READY FOR A GAME.

CHESSBOARD TABLE

Ajunk-shop find, this glass-topped table will double for dining as well as chess. With the design on the underside of the glass, the top surface is still practical and easily cleaned, but totally transformed. This method of decorating glass is known as backpainting, and it means that the finest details – in this case, the veins of the marble – must be painted first. Although it is a large project, this is a simple basic method, so try it out on something small first, and then enjoy planning the design to co-ordinate with your own chess set.

MATERIALS & EQUIPMENT

- Plain and squared paper
- Pencil
- Scissors
- Felt-tipped pen
- Straight-edge
- Glue
- Photocopier
- Masking tape
- Lint-free cloth
- Washing-up liquid
- Artist's acrylic paints
- Fine paintbrush
- Acrylic outline paste
- Paper towels
- Craft knife
- Soft paintbrush
- Glass paints and solvent
- Water-based polyurethane varnish (optional)
- 9mm adhesive lead (optional)

TECHNIQUE FOCUS

Marbled paint finish
see *page 23*

Preparing the design
see *page 24*

Applying acrylic outline
paste see *page 26*

ONE Use plain paper to make a template of the table, cut out and fold in half and then in quarters. With a pen, mark the quarters clearly along the folded creases.

TWO On a piece of squared paper, mark out the chessboard itself, fold to find the quarters, centre it on the basic template and glue in place.

THREE Now choose the border and any other motifs you wish to add. Make photocopies of any repeating pattern, cut them out and use these to build up the design. Tape in position when you are happy with the arrangement.

FOUR This table had a detachable glass top which was simple to lift off. You may need to find another way to work on your table, but remember to paint on the underside. Lay the finished design face up and position the glass over it. Tape in place with masking tape. Clean any fingermarks with a lint-free cloth and dilute washing-up liquid, then avoid touching the glass if possible.

FIVE Start by painting the veins to give the effect of marble, using acrylic paints and a fine paintbrush, and allow to dry. Outline the chessboard area in the centre with acrylic outline paste, using a long straight-edge. Hold the tube at a slight angle to the straight-edge, so that

the paste is not smudged. Squeeze the paste out evenly doing all the vertical lines first. Allow to dry thoroughly. Turn through 90° and do all the horizontal lines. When dry trim any excess paste and over runs with a craft knife. Finish by tracing the border and then the decorative motifs. Allow to dry and remove the paper template.

SIX Using a soft paintbrush, paint the design generously with glass paint. The paint will seal in the acrylic marble effect. Remember the painted surface will be the underside. Allow to harden off for a day, then turn the glass top over and position it on the frame. For that finishing touch, we added 9mm adhesive lead right round the edge of the table, then rubbed it down with a boning peg.

DESIGN DIRECTORY

FLORAL SCROLL BORDER

WITH THE DESIGN ON THE UNDERSIDE OF THE GLASS,
THE TOP SURFACEIS EASILY CLEANED AND PRACTICAL

WORLD ART BORDER

DRAGON AND PICTISH KNOTWORK

CUPBOARD DOORS WITH CHERRIES

These delightful cherries transform an ordinary glass-fronted kitchen cupboard. The glass 'jewel' fruits add a fascinating sparkle to the surface decoration. Adapt the design as necessary to fit your own kitchen furniture. Using adhesive materials, it is easy to make the design without taking the door off its hinges.

MATERIALS & EQUIPMENT

- Carbon paper
- Coloured transparent adhesive film
- Design template
- Masking tape
- Coloured ballpoint pen
- Scissors
- Water spray with dilute washing-up liquid
- Squeegee
- Glass 'jewels'
- Coarse sandpaper
- Fast-setting two-part clear epoxy resin glue
- Toothpick
- Scrap of card
- Lightweight household or gardening gloves
- Twin strand adhesive lead
- Old scissors
- Small chisel
- Boning peg (or ballpoint pen with lid)

ONE Place a sheet of carbon paper face down over the coloured film. Position the design template over the carbon paper and tape in place. Use the coloured ballpoint pen to trace the leaves onto the film. Remove the template. To avoid confusion, cut out each leaf only when you are ready to fix it in place. Position the design template inside the cupboard, facing into the room.

TWO Cut out the first piece of film. To apply, spray the clean glass with a weak solution of washing-up liquid. Peel the backing off the piece of film and slide it into place. It will move freely on the glass. When you are satisfied with the position, carefully remove excess water with the squeegee. Complete the rest of the design in the same way and allow to dry out thoroughly (about 2 hours).

THREE The 'jewels' should be glued in place next. Using coarse sandpaper, roughen the areas where the cherries are to be positioned and also

TECHNIQUE FOCUS

Preparing the design
see page 24

Adhesive lead and coloured adhesive film *see page 32*

Applying 'jewels'
see page 35

the base of the cherries. Following the manufacturer's instructions, apply a little epoxy resin glue to the base of each 'jewel' and stick it in place. Secure with masking tape until the glue has hardened (about 5 minutes).

FOUR Finish with the lead outline. Wearing gloves to protect your hands, separate the strands of lead by making a small cut into the end with the chisel and pulling them apart. Apply the lead strips following the sequence of numbers given on the design, so that all loose lead ends are secured as the work proceeds. Make sure that the lead covers the edge of the film, leaving no loose edges.

FIVE Burnish the lead when you are satisfied with its position, using the boning peg. Take special care to rub down any points where two pieces of lead cross one another. Run the peg carefully along the full length of each piece, to ensure that it has adhered to the glass effectively. Remove the paper template.

DESIGN DIRECTORY

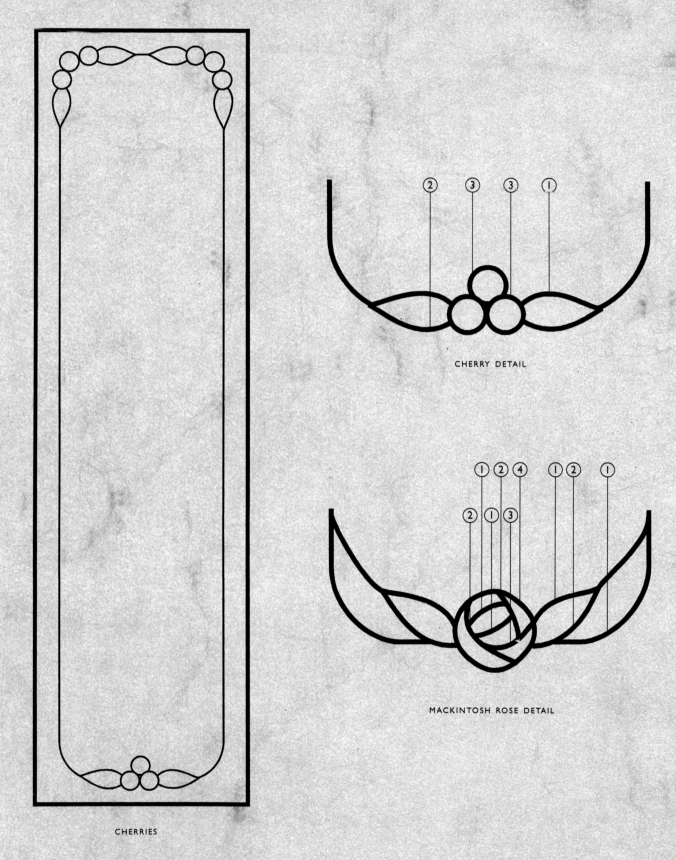

CHERRY DETAIL

MACKINTOSH ROSE DETAIL

CHERRIES

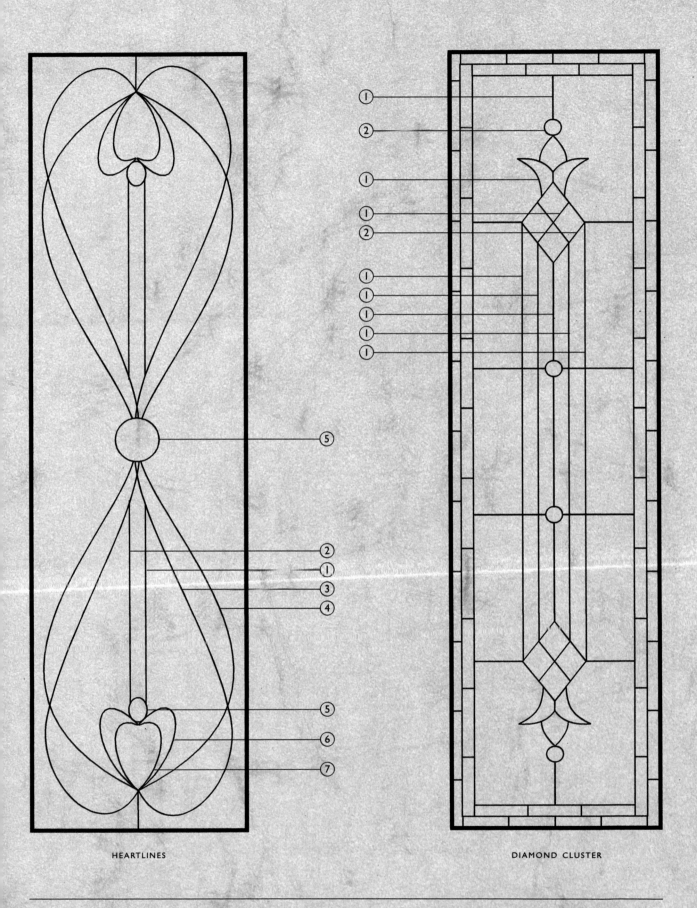

HEARTLINES

DIAMOND CLUSTER

ETCHED STARS & STRIPES

If you are intrigued by the beautiful frosted appearance of etched glass you can now produce it for yourself: try out the technique on a small project like this first. Self-adhesive shapes are easy to use and get you away to a good start. Decorate a jug and glasses for cool summer drinks in the garden, or some storage jars for the kitchen.

MATERIALS & EQUIPMENT

- Glass
- Washing-up liquid
- Paper towels
- Electrical insulating tape
- Self-adhesive stars
- Rubber gloves
- Fitch brush or small decorator's paintbrush
- Etching paste

ONE Prepare the item to be etched. Wash in dilute washing-up liquid and dry with paper towels.

TWO Mask off the areas that are to remain shiny. Apply strips of electrical insulating tape diagonally around the glass to create a spiral pattern. Fill the spaces between the tape strips with rows of stars. (Adhesive shapes may be purchased at good stationers. Try spots for polka dots, linen

TECHNIQUE FOCUS

Etching glass see *page 34*

reinforcing rings or even letters for names.) Avoid handling the glass too much as fingermarks will slow up the etching process.

THREE Wear rubber gloves to apply the paste and work in a well ventilated area. Use a fitch brush to apply the paste, covering the glass quite thickly.

FOUR Leave for about an hour or for the time recommended by the manufacturer, then wash off with copious amounts of water. Different types of glass will be etched at differing rates so you may need to repeat the process before removing the adhesive stars and tape. Clean the work area thoroughly. Remove the stars and stripes with a small knife under hot water if necessary. Wash the glasses and once thoroughly dry, they are ready for use.

CAUTION

Take common-sense precautions to prevent accidents. Work in a workshop or shed with no interruptions or children about, as the paste contains acid. Wear rubber gloves and put down polythene to catch any drips. Make sure you have ready access to a water supply and the area is well ventilated. Follow the manufacturer's recommendations carefully and lock the paste away immediately after use.

TIFFANY POPPY

DECO HEART FRIEZE

MAKE A PAPER PATTERN OF YOUR LIGHT FITTING,
AND ADAPT THE DESIGN TO FIT.

MORNING GLORY

KINGFISHER WINDOW TO MASK A POOR VIEW

If your back door or window gives onto an unattractive view, make the glorious colours of the kingfisher the focus of attention instead. Use clear colours so that you can still see through it, or a textured background to give privacy. Choose the method best suited to the situation. It could also be done with the lead outline on back and front, or made into a double glazed unit, for durability, to replace an existing window. Alternatively, the design could be made in lead with adhesive coloured film on the inside of the window, or a second pane could be decorated and added to the existing window using wooden moulding to hold it in place. Here the design has been worked in adhesive lead, with outliner and paint on the reverse.

MATERIALS & EQUIPMENT

- Design template
- Glass or plastic sheet
- Lint-free cloth
- Masking tape
- Lightweight household or gardening gloves
- Twin strand adhesive lead
- Old scissors
- Small chisel
- Boning peg (or ballpoint pen with lid)
- Acrylic outline paste
- Paper towels
- Craft knife
- Soft paintbrush
- Glass paints and solvent

ONE Make a paper pattern of your door, and centre the motif within it. Add a border to suit your individual window (see Preparing the Design, page 24). Here we added a lattice lead grid to an oval border for a cottagey effect.

TWO Lay the template design face up and position the clean glass over it. Tape in place with masking tape. Consider the 'route' for the lead outline. Wearing gloves, add the lead strips following the sequence of numbers given on the design, so that all loose ends are secured as the work proceeds.

THREE Burnish the lead when you are satisfied with its position, using the boning peg. Take special care to rub down any points where two pieces of lead cross one another. Run the peg carefully along the full length of each piece, to

TECHNIQUE FOCUS

Large areas; textured paint finishes; using white paint see *page 21, 23*

Preparing the design see *page 24*

Lead outline with paste and paint on back see *page 28*

ensure that it has adhered to the glass effectively. Remove the paper template.

FOUR Turn the glass over and clean well. Using acrylic outline paste, follow the lead outline. Allow to dry (about 10 minutes).

FIVE Using a soft paintbrush, paint the design generously with glass paint, lifting the glass to check that the paint is even. Allow the paintbrush onto the outline, as you paint. This will help to seal the outline.

DESIGN DIRECTORY

NUMBERS INDICATE THE ORDER OF WORKING WITH LEAD OUTLINE

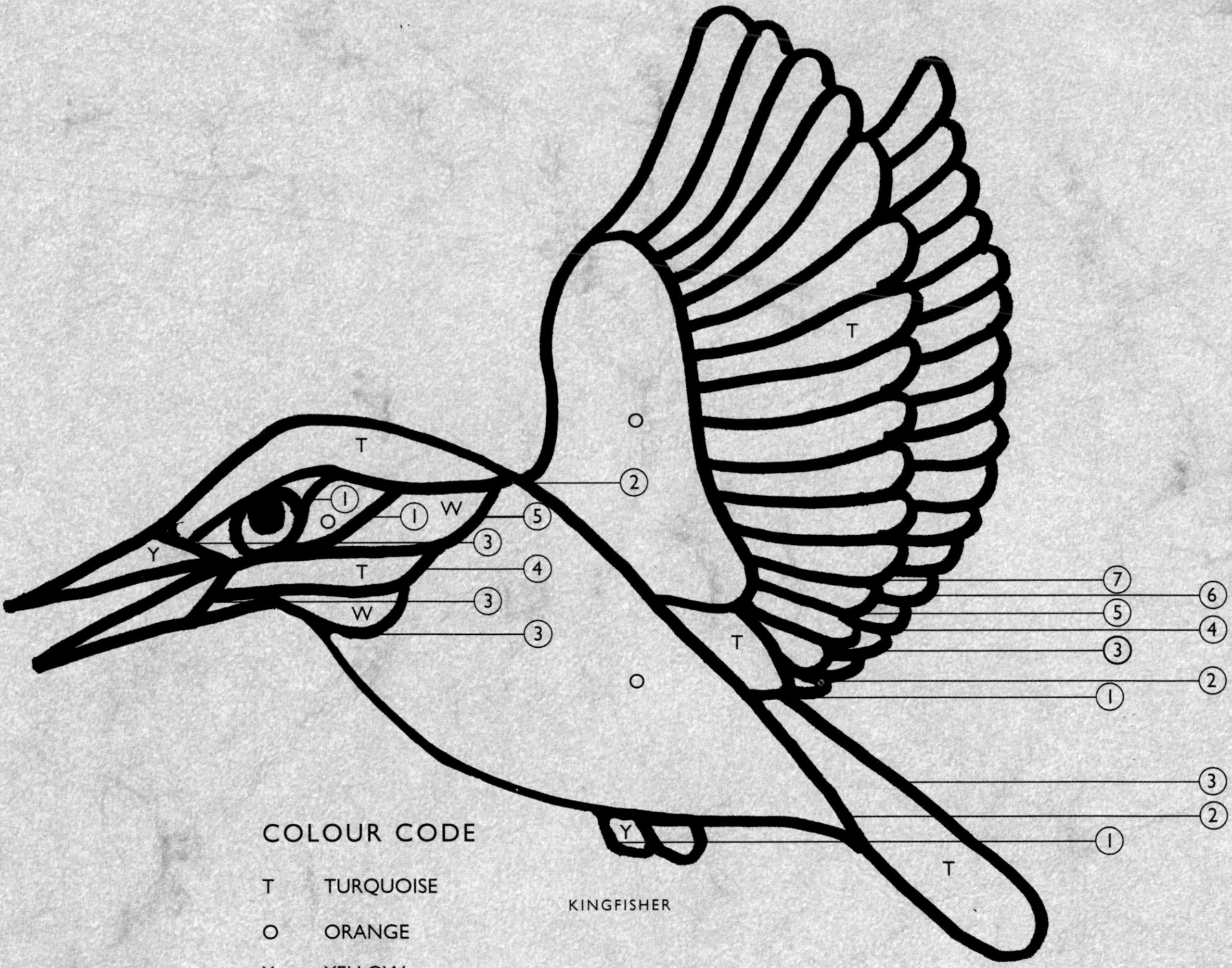

KINGFISHER

COLOUR CODE

T	TURQUOISE
O	ORANGE
Y	YELLOW
W	WHITE

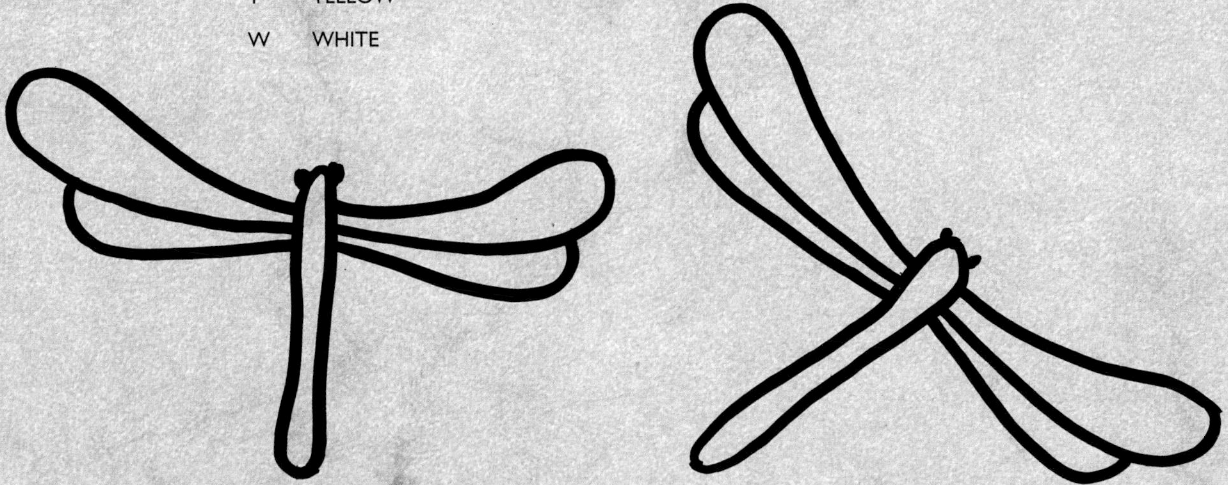

DRAGONFLIES

FRUIT BASKET

FIVE ACRE WOOD

BEDROOM

AWAY FROM THE MORE PUBLIC ROOMS IN THE HOME, YOU
ARE FREE TO HAVE SOME GLASS PAINTING FUN WITH A
DELIGHTFUL TEDDY'S CASTLE BEDHEAD FOR A CHILD, OR
ADD A LITTLE MAGIC TO A MIRROR, OR DREAM AWHILE WITH
THE SOFT CANDLE-LIGHT REFLECTED IN THE MIRRORED
CANDLE SCONCE. WE SCOURED THE SECOND-HAND SHOPS
FOR MANY OF OUR OWN FAVOURITE PIECES, INCLUDING AN
ORIGINAL FIFTIES KIDNEY DRESSING TABLE, WITH A TRIPLE
MIRROR, AND ALL THE GLASS INTACT. A CLASSIC LIKE THIS
WILL RESPOND TO ANY DECORATIVE DESIGN TREATMENT, A
FEATURE IN ITSELF, FOR A TEENAGER OR FOR A MASTER
BEDROOM.

TEDDIES' CASTLE

TEMPLATE FOR BASIC HEADBOARD SHAPE

TEMPLATES FOR ACRYLIC WINDOWS

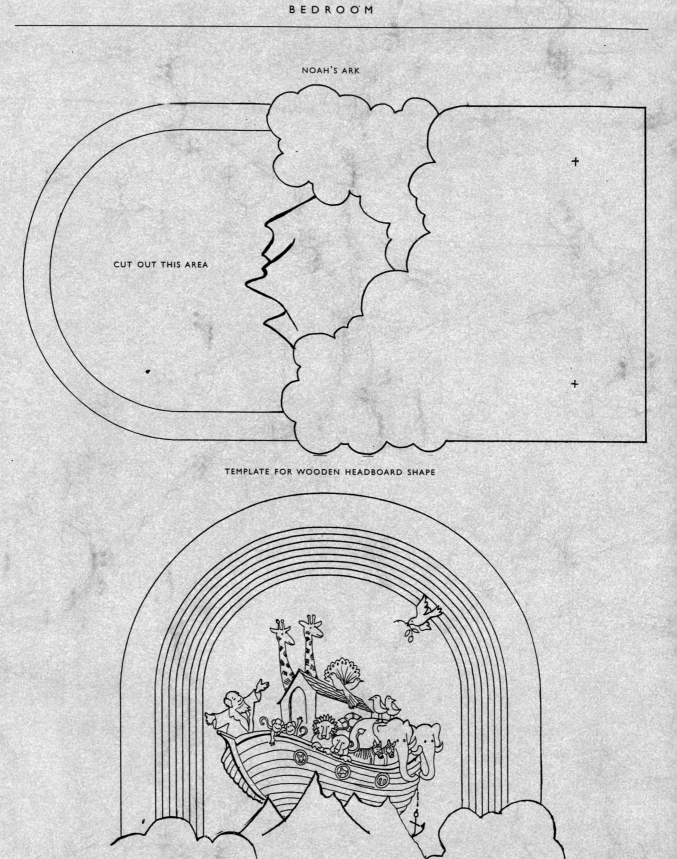

NOAH'S ARK

CUT OUT THIS AREA

TEMPLATE FOR WOODEN HEADBOARD SHAPE

TEMPLATE FOR ACRYLIC SHEET SHOWING PART OF THE WOODEN HEADBOARD

FAIRY GROTTO

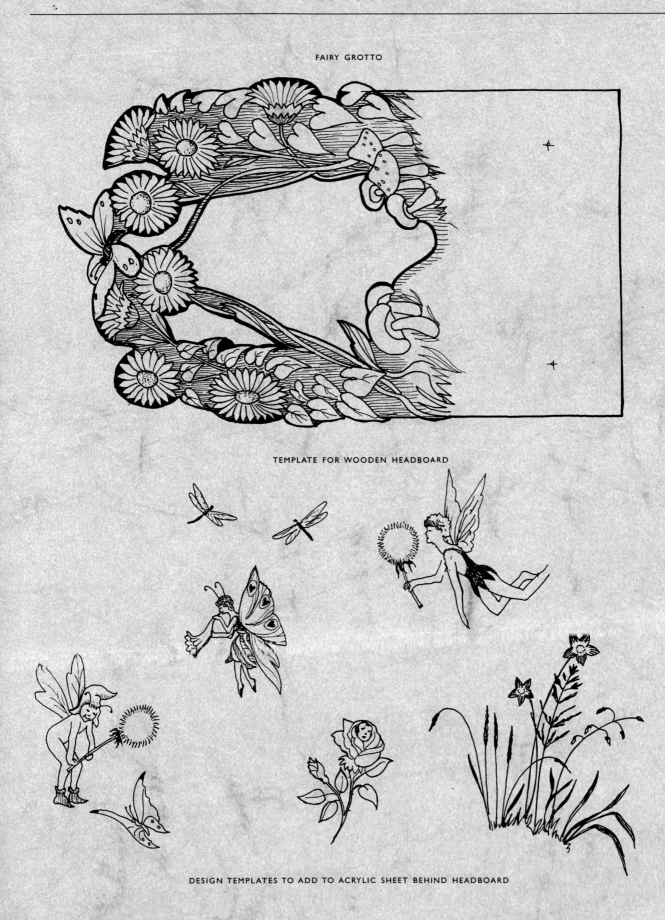

TEMPLATE FOR WOODEN HEADBOARD

DESIGN TEMPLATES TO ADD TO ACRYLIC SHEET BEHIND HEADBOARD

TURKISH-STYLE BEDROOM MIRROR

Your chance to play with the materials – pure self-indulgence! A junk shop find, this sixties mirror is well made, with a deep frame just right for lining with mosaic. Make sure the mirror you choose is large enough to carry this sort of decoration and still leave a usable area.

MATERIALS & EQUIPMENT

- Scrap mirror pieces 2mm thick
- Glass cutter
- Metal straight-edge
- Pliers
- Ceramic wall tile adhesive
- Damp and dry cloths
- Sandpaper
- Tile grout
- Old paintbrush
- Strong plain paper and pencil
- Scissors
- Felt-tipped pens
- Acrylic outline paste
- Paper towels
- Craft knife
- Soft paintbrush
- Glass paints and solvent
- Small star stencil
- Sponge

CAUTION

Care must be taken when cutting glass. Cover the work surface with newspaper to catch glass slivers, to be disposed of safely. Glass-cutting is best done in a shed or garage, away from food preparation areas and the family.

ONE To make the mosaic pieces for the frame, cut the mirror into strips using a glass cutter and metal straight-edge. Score the strips and break into small squares with the pliers. Using tile adhesive, cover the frame with mosaic pieces. Wipe with a damp cloth to remove excess adhesive before it dries. Leave overnight to dry.

TWO With the sandpaper, rub down any sharp edges. Mix up some tile grout and work it into the gaps using an old paintbrush, wiping away any excess while still damp. Leave to dry for about 40 minutes. Use a damp cloth to clean up the mirror and then polish with a dry cloth.

THREE Make a paper pattern of the mirror, fold it in half and mark the centre. With the paper still folded in half, sketch the border shape and cut it out to make a template. Open flat and centre this template on the mirror. With a felt-tipped pen, draw round the edge of the template, marking the border onto the mirror. Remove the template, fold it in half as before and mark the second border 2.5cm (1in) smaller all round. Cut away the 2.5cm (1in) wide strip, open the template out flat and reposition it on the glass. With the felt-tipped pen, mark the second border

TECHNIQUE FOCUS

Painting large areas
see page 21

Preparing the design
see page 24

Applying acrylic outline paste see page 26

on the mirror. Remove the template. Cut out paper stars, place in position on the mirror and draw round them as for the border. Remove the templates.

FOUR With the outline paste, follow the felt-tip lines to draw the double border and stars. Allow to dry for 20 minutes.

FIVE Stick further pieces of mosaic on the diagonal like diamonds within the main border. Clean up and allow to dry as before.

SIX With a soft paintbrush, apply turquoise glass paint generously to the whole border area but leaving the stars clear. Work quickly, keeping the paint moving, so that there is no time for a 'tide line' to form. Paint the inner border, including the mosaic edges, in magenta or purple. Allow to dry for 30 minutes.

SEVEN Using silver paste, outline the borders and stars and add details such as the row of dots around the border. The tiny stars are stencilled, using silver paste on a small sponge. This could also be used to paint the edges of the frame. As a final touch, add random dots of silver over the entire border area.

DESIGN DIRECTORY

TURKISH DELIGHT

HEART THROB

THE BUBBLE FAIRY

ROSE DRESSING TABLE & TRIPLE MIRROR

This classic piece was found in a sad corner of a second-hand shop. With a lot of love and a little patience it has come back to life as the charming focal point of our guest room. Here we are faced with both transparent glass and mirrored surfaces, so we decided to treat both the same way, as mirror. The design is made with lead on the glass surface, which offers an exciting surface texture to the piece.

MATERIALS & EQUIPMENT

- Design template
- Masking tape
- Lint-free cloth
- Washing-up liquid
- Glass paints and solvent
- Soft paintbrush
- Paper towels
- Carbon paper
- Coloured ballpoint pen
- Lightweight household or gardening gloves
- Twin strand adhesive lead
- Old scissors
- Small chisel
- Boning peg (or ballpoint pen with lid)

PRACTICAL TIP.

Rub down and paint the dressing table according to the style that you want to achieve. You may wish to apply a decorative acrylic finish at this stage.

ONE Lay the design template face up and position the glass table-top over it. Tape in place with masking tape. Clean any fingermarks with a lint-free cloth and dilute washing-up liquid, then avoid touching the glass if possible.

TWO Mix a little white glass paint into the colour to give the paint enough body to be seen against an opaque background. Using a soft paintbrush, paint the design on the glass table-top. Leave narrow gaps between the blocks of colour and allow each colour to dry for 5 minutes before applying the adjacent one.

THREE Using carbon paper and a coloured ballpoint pen, transfer the design onto the triple mirror. Paint in the same way, leaving narrow gaps between the blocks of colour. Allow the paint on both table-top and mirror to harden for at least 3 days.

FOUR Consider the 'route' for the lead

TECHNIQUE FOCUS

Lead outline on a painted surface see *page 28*

Mirrors; using white paint see *page 23*

outline. Wearing gloves to handle the lead, add the lead strips following the sequence of numbers given on the design, so that all loose ends are secured as the work proceeds. Burnish the lead when you are satisfied with its position, using the boning peg. Take special care to rub down any points where two pieces of lead cross one another. Run the peg carefully along the full length of each piece, to ensure that it has adhered to the glass effectively.

PRACTICAL TIP

We painted a second colour over the flowers and leaves to enhance them. If you want to do this, allow the first coat to harden off well beforehand.

DESIGN DIRECTORY

NUMBERS INDICATE THE ORDER OF WORKING WITH LEAD OUTLINE

ALLOW THE PAINT TO HARDEN FOR SEVERAL DAYS
BEFORE APPLYING THE LEAD OUTLINE OVER IT

MACKINTOSH-STYLE ROSES

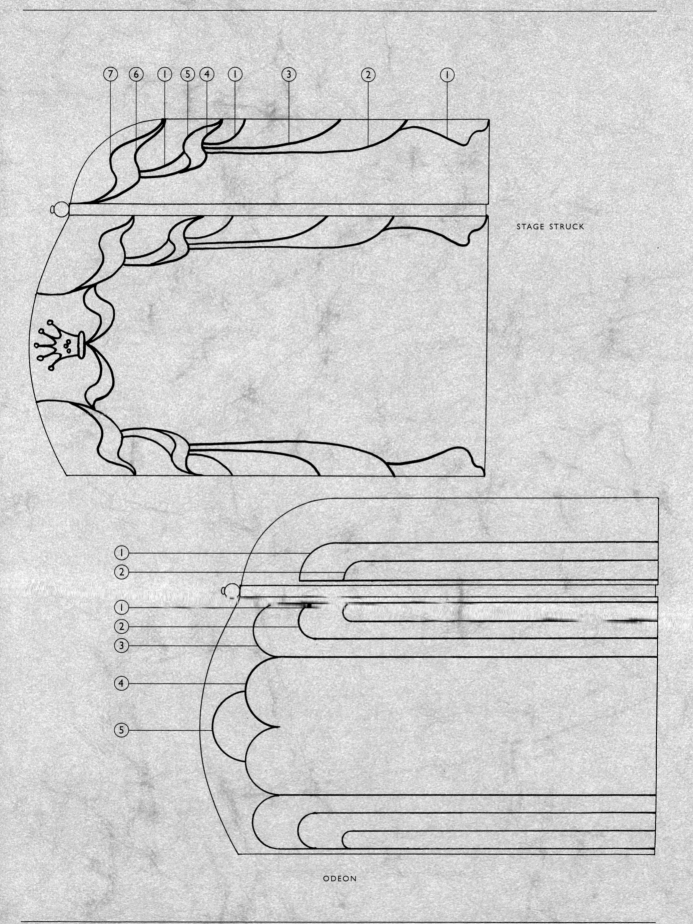

STAGE STRUCK

ODEON

CANDLE SCONCE WITH MIRROR MOSAIC

A sparkling candle sconce becomes the perfect focus for a romantic room. Create a dreamy space where you can drift gently away or relax with a glass of wine and a good book. This lovely project is surprisingly simple, and will give much pleasure. A bathroom could also be a perfect setting for the soft, flickering light of the oil lamp. Even when the lamp is not lit, the candle sconce twinkles with reflected light.

MATERIALS & EQUIPMENT

- Metal straight-edge
- Glass cutter
- Thick gloves
- Scrap 2mm mirror pieces
- Pliers
- Wooden candle sconce, preferably hinged
- Ceramic wall tile adhesive
- Damp and dry cloths
- Sandpaper
- White tile grout
- Old paintbrush
- Acrylic paint
- Paintbrush
- Acrylic outline paste in gold

ONE Using a straight-edge and glass cutter, make strips of mirror about 1cm (½in) wide. Slight variations will add to the character of the mosaic. Take one strip at a time and, using the glass cutter, score across the strips at varying widths and angles. Break the strips carefully with a pair of pliers to create the pieces of mosaic.

TWO Ensure the wood sconce is dry and free from grease or dust. Consider whether you need to remove any metal fittings from the sconce, to give a flat area for the mosaic. Spread an area 15cm (6in) square with tile adhesive, following the manufacturer's instructions. The adhesive should be quite thickly spread to allow the mirror pieces to lie at different angles, to pick up more twinkling light.

THREE Starting from the edges, work inwards, placing the glass pieces one at a time and leaving small gaps between them. Spread more adhesive until the mosaic is complete. Wipe off any excess adhesive with a damp cloth before it dries. Leave for about 24 hours to dry.

FOUR With the sandpaper, carefully rub down any sharp edges. Mix up a small quantity of tile grout to a creamy consistency and, using an old paintbrush, work the grout over the entire surface. While still workable remove some of the excess with a damp cloth. Allow to dry for about 40 minutes.

FIVE When dry, clean up with a dryish cloth. Clean the edges and around the hinges again with sandpaper. The mirror may now be polished with a dry cloth. Replace any metal fittings removed earlier.

SIX For an attractive finish, paint the wooden edges with acrylic paint (we used blue-green to look like verdigris) and decorate them with gold outline paste, which you can also use to cover the grouting. Any leftover pieces of mosaic could be used to decorate jars, mirror frames or boxes to match the sconce.

CAUTION

Care must be taken when cutting glass. Cover the work surface with newspaper to catch glass slivers, to be disposed of safely. Glass-cutting is best done in a shed or garage, away from food preparation areas and the family.

AUTUMN LEAVES
TO LIFT A DULL VIEW

As an alternative to a net curtain, these windswept leaves offer as much privacy as you need, while bringing life and colour to a view from a side window. This is a study window, but you could also try it with stars or hearts for a teenage bedroom. It couldn't be easier: the leaves are simply cut from adhesive film and used with no outline. Overlap the film to mix the colours. Stick the leaves directly onto the window, or to a sheet of clear plastic which can be fixed to the existing window with double-sided tape.

TECHNIQUE FOCUS

Coloured adhesive film
see page 32

MATERIALS & EQUIPMENT

• Carbon paper
• Coloured transparent adhesive film in several related colours
• Design template
• Masking tape
• Coloured ballpoint pen
• Scissors
• Glass or plastic sheet
• Water spray with dilute washing-up liquid
• Squeegee, for removing excess water

ONE Place a sheet of carbon paper face down over the coloured film. Position the design template over the carbon paper and tape in place. Use a coloured ballpoint pen to trace the design onto the film. Remove the design and repeat the process for each colour film.

TWO Spray the glass or plastic with a weak solution of washing-up liquid. Cut out the first leaf and apply it to the glass or plastic. When you are satisfied with its position, carefully remove excess water with a squeegee. Build up a random design with leaves of different colours and shapes, until the view is sufficiently obscured. If you are using a sheet of plastic, add leaves to both sides of the sheet, overlapping to mix the colours. Allow to dry out thoroughly.

DESIGN DIRECTORY

AUTUMN LEAVES

CONFETTI

PETALS

SWIFTS

BATHROOM

WHO WOULD THINK THAT EVEN A BATHROOM COULD BENEFIT FROM THE ATTENTION OF A CREATIVE EYE? GIVEN TIME TO HARDEN OFF PROPERLY, GOOD QUALITY GLASS PAINTS ARE EVEN EQUAL TO THE DELIGHTFUL JOB OF DECORATING TILES. WE PLAYED WITH ETCHED AND STENCILLED FINISHES TOO FOR THE MERMAID SHOWER SCREEN AND THE FROSTED WINDOW. MANY COMMERCIALLY PRODUCED STENCILS ARE NOW AVAILABLE SO THE CHOICE OF DESIGNS OPEN TO YOU IS ENDLESS.

MERMAID SHOWER SCREEN

The family bathroom, away from the public eye, is a perfect place to try out ideas. Most shower screens are made of toughened glass, though some may be acrylic. Obviously, only a glass screen can be etched, but it is possible to decorate acrylic too. Instructions are given here for etching a glass screen which of course is permanent, but the mermaid design could be used with adhesive film. Try it in white film without the lead outline, to give an impression of etched glass, or in full glorious colour, but remember to keep the individual pieces of film small: larger areas are tricky.

TECHNIQUE FOCUS

Etching glass see *page 34*

MATERIALS & EQUIPMENT

- Shower screen
- Self-adhesive vinyl sheet
- Masking tape
- Design template
- Carbon paper
- Coloured ballpoint pen
- Craft knife
- Rubber gloves
- Etching paste
- Fitch brush or small decorator's paintbrush

PRACTICAL TIP

You might like to etch some small designs on the other side of the glass, to create more interest.

ONE Dismantle the screen sufficiently to lay it flat in an area where etching materials are safe to use on this scale. Stick the adhesive vinyl over the area to be decorated. If necessary, enlarge the designs on a photocopier and experiment until you are happy with the layout. Use masking tape to secure the design template lightly and slip carbon paper underneath with the carbon side face down. Using a coloured ballpoint pen, trace the design onto the adhesive vinyl. Remove the design and carbon paper.

C A U T I O N

Take common-sense precautions to prevent accidents. Work in a workshop or shed with no interruptions or children about, as the paste contains acid. Wear rubber gloves and put down polythene to catch any drips. Make sure you have ready access to a water supply and the area is well ventilated. Follow the manufacturer's recommendations carefully and lock the paste away immediately after use.

TWO Using a craft knife, carefully cut around the design and peel away the areas to be etched. Wearing rubber gloves, apply the etching paste according to the manufacturer's instructions. After 20 minutes, rinse off the paste and dry the glass. If the etching is still patchy apply the paste a second time. When you are happy with the effect, peel off the vinyl and wash the screen thoroughly.

MERMAID

JAPANESE SEA WAVE

DOLPHINS

OBSCURED BATHROOM WINDOW

An attractive and practical print on this window allows light into the room, while offering privacy. A charming lacy pattern gives a traditional effect, but why not try the spirals, stars or Japanese vine? Pre-cut stencils are available from DIY and craft suppliers, and they could be used to build up the effect of an overall etched design. This method will work for any window which cannot be laid flat.

MATERIALS & EQUIPMENT

- Self-adhesive vinyl sheet
- Masking tape
- Design template
- Carbon paper
- Coloured ballpoint pen
- Craft knife
- 2.5cm (1in) cubes of plastic foam
- Glass paints and solvent, or frosting equipment
- Paint container

PRACTICAL TIP

Try this project on a warm day to avoid condensation. Allow the paint to harden off for 3 days before cleaning it.

ONE Smooth the adhesive vinyl onto the clean glass. Use a little masking tape to fix the design template over the vinyl. Slip some carbon paper under the paper template, with the carbon side face down. Trace the design onto the vinyl using a coloured ballpoint pen. Remove the carbon paper and template.

TWO Cut along the outline using a craft knife. Peel away the vinyl from the parts which are to be painted. The glass will remain clear where the vinyl is left while you apply colour.

THREE Pinch the top of a foam cube together and wind masking tape round it to make a handle. Mix a little white glass paint with clear glass paint, dip the sponge into it and practise printing on a scrap of glass or plastic sheet. When you are satisfied with the effect, mix up enough paint for the whole area and print the window. Allow to dry for 20 minutes or until the paint is just touch dry.

FOUR Carefully peel away the remaining vinyl.

DESIGN DIRECTORY

MEDIEVAL PRINT

SPIRALS

STARDUST

JAPANESE VINE

BATHROOM TILES

What fun we had with this project! These are simply standard low-glaze white tiles from a DIY store. The silly fish are really jolly, but why not try a stylish deco theme? Test out the quality of your paints on a single tile, before committing yourself to a whole room-full. In an ideal world it would be better to paint the tiles before fixing them to the wall. However if your bathroom is already tiled, you could remove a few random ones by carefully chipping them out with a cold chisel and replace with hand painted ones. The mirror mosaic method could also be used to fill the place of a tile.

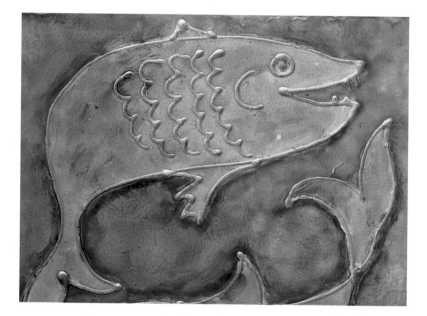

TECHNIQUE FOCUS

Painting tiles *see page 22*

THREE Select the paint colours you wish to use. Using a soft paintbrush, cover the entire tile with clear paint, going over the outline and right to the edges, so that when the paint hardens the design will be waterproof and wipeable. Add the other colours carefully to the clear paint while it is still wet. Add either more clear or more of the colour to control the depth of colour. Work on one tile at a time, before moving on to the next one. Leave to harden off for at least 3 days before allowing the tiles to get wet.

MATERIALS & EQUIPMENT

- Design template
- Plain, low-glaze white tiles
- Carbon paper
- Masking tape
- Coloured ballpoint pen
- Tube of acrylic outline paste
- Paper towels
- Craft knife
- Glass paints, including clear paint, and solvent
- Soft paintbrush

ONE Position the design template with the design face up over a clean tile. Slip a sheet of carbon paper under the template with the carbon side face downwards. Secure with a little masking tape. Use a coloured ballpoint pen to mark the design onto the tile. Remove the template and carbon paper.

TWO Use acrylic outline paste to draw the design onto the tile. Gold or silver are particularly effective. You may find a hairdryer useful when working on a vertical surface.

DESIGN DIRECTORY

SEASHELLS

FUNNY FISH

GEOMETRIC FLOWER TILE

DECO TILE

GENERAL SUPPLIERS

CRAFT & ART SHOPS acrylic outliners, glass paints, paint brushes, stencils for etching

DIY & HARDWARE SHOPS adhesive lead, boning peg, brush cleaners and solvents, coloured film, grate polish or lead blacking, grid and lattice design guides, plastic sheet, low glaze plain white tiles. Also glass and double glazing products, inc. silica crystals

GLAZIERS glass and double glazing products, including silica crystals

COMPUTER DESIGN PACKAGES For example GSP Designworks, KeyCAD, Coreldraw, TurboCAD or Microsoft Paintbrush, see specialist magazines

USEFUL ADDRESSES

Designs In Wood,
Unit 8, Haleacre Farm,
Watchet Lane, Little Kingshill,
Buckinghamshire HP16 0DR
Tel: 01494 866669
MDF blanks

Kansa Craft,
The Old Flour Mill, Wath Road,
Elsecar, Barnsley, South Yorkshire
S74 8HW
Tel: 01226 747424
etching paste, professional quality jewels, glass bead fringing

ICI Paints,
Wexham Road, Slough SL2 5DS
Tel: 01753 550555
varnish

Lead and Light,
35a Hartland Road, Camden,
London NW1 8DB
Tel: 0171 485 0997
etching paste, professional quality jewels, glass bead fringing

Tempsford Stained Glass,
The Old School, Tempsford, Nr
Sandy, Bedfordshire SG19
Tel: 01767 640235
etching paste, professional quality jewels, glass bead fringing

The Glass Painting Specialists,
48 Coningsby Road, High
Wycombe, Buckinghamshire

HP13 5NY
Tel: 01494 528785
professional quality glass paints, lead and adhesive coloured film

C&R Loo, Inc.
1085 Essex Avenue, Richmond, CA
94801
Tel: (510) 232-0276
Toll Free, US & Canada: (800) 227-1780
Fax: (510) 232-7810
Website: http://www.crloo.com

Ed Hoy's International
1620 Frontenac Road
Naperville, IL 60563
Tel: (630) 420-0890
Toll Free, US & Canada: (800) 323-5668
Fax: (630) 416-0448
Website: http://www.edhoy.com

Franklin Art Glass Studios, Inc.
222 E. Sycamore Street
Columbus, OH 43206
Tel: (614) 221-2972
Toll Free: (800) 848-7683
Fax: (614) 221-5223

Houston Stained Glass Supply
2002 Brittmoore Road
Houston, TX 77403-2209
Tel: (713) 690-8844
Toll Free: (800) 231-0148
Fax: (713) 690-0009
Website: http://www.hsgs.com

Hudson Glass Co., Inc.
219 N. Division Street
Peekskill, NY 10566-2700
Tel: (914) 737-2124
Toll Free: (800) 431-2964
Fax: (914) 737-4447

Jurgen Industries, Inc.
14700 172nd Drive, SE#1
Monroe, WA 98272
Tel: (360) 794-7886
Fax: (360) 794-9825
Website:
http://www.jurgenindustries.com

Meredith Stained Glass Center, Inc.
1115 East-West Highway
Silver Spring, MD 20910
Tel: (301) 953-1740
Toll Free: (800) 966-6667
Website: http://www.meredithglass.com

United Art Glass, Inc.
1032 East Ogden Avenue #128
Naperville, IL 60563-2839
Tel: (630) 369-8168
Orders: (800) 323-9760

Whittemore-Durgin Glass Co.
P.O. Box 2065 NN
Hanover, MA 02339
Tel: (781) 871-1790
Toll Free: (800) 225-0380
Fax: (800) 786-3457
Website:
http://www.penrose.com/glass/

INDEX